EBURY PRESS
ROOH

Born in Baramulla, Kashmir, Manav Kaul has been an integral part of the film world, acting, directing and writing for the past twenty years. With each of his new plays, Manav has made people sit up and take notice, and he has created an equally valuable body of work as a writer. His books *Theek Tumhare Peeche* (Right Behind You) and *Prem Kabootar* (Love Pigeon) have been dominating the Nielsen bestseller list.

T0006666

Celebrating 35 Years of
Penguin Random House India

A NOVEL

MANAV KAUL

**EBURY
PRESS**

An imprint of Penguin Random House

EBURY PRESS

USA | Canada | UK | Ireland | Australia
New Zealand | India | South Africa | China

Ebury Press is part of the Penguin Random House group of companies
whose addresses can be found at global.penguinrandomhouse.com

Published by Penguin Random House India Pvt. Ltd
4th Floor, Capital Tower 1, MG Road,
Gurugram 122 002, Haryana, India

First published in Ebury Press by Penguin Random House India 2023

Copyright © Manav Kaul 2023

Translated from the Hindi by Pooja Priyamvada

All rights reserved

10 9 8 7 6 5 4 3 2 1

ISBN 9780143462460

Typeset in Garamond by MAP Systems, Bengaluru, India

www.penguin.co.in

Author's Note

That Which Was Never to Be Written

This was the book that I never wanted to write. Even in the process of writing it I was aware that I wasn't really writing it. It was more like a ruse—I was on a trip, I was a traveller, and I was recording the experiences of my travels. I've always been muddle-headed. My paths to arrive at a sentence are often quite jagged. At times I feel I am a mathematician with an equation developing inside of me that I am constantly trying to solve. But each time I complete a book, I feel as if I have resolved nothing—just tried to make sense of the equation from different points of view.

I have been working on my equation with Kashmir since childhood. My dialogues about Kashmir have always fascinated me, but I've never had the courage to put them in order in one place. Somewhere inside I was afraid as to what it could all mean—all these dialogues, that seemed so personal, sounded artificial to me.

Our childhood has been abundant and prosperous, and the vignettes from that past are personal to each one of us, but we think highly of those who are experts in the art of telling tales about their childhood. Yet I was, in a way, avoiding using my storytelling ability in relation to my childhood and hence never wanted to write this book. Then I looked back at whatever I had written before, and it occurred to me that all of that was imaginary; what I was trying to escape from was actually my real writing. I am a writer, and I invite people into an imaginary world that I create. The day I understood this was the day the first sentences of this book germinated in my mind.

When I first reached Kashmir to write this book in all my immaturity, I could only see a dry, rocky ground where no writing was possible. While walking on those rugged paths, whichever stone I upturned I found life, dewiness and love beneath it. I have never walked cautiously. I keep recording what I encounter as it is, and along with it, the life I would like to see. Sometimes I think I wanted to write about my father and I wrote about Kashmir, and when I sat down to write about Kashmir, I saw my father.

All my memories are of the times when things were tangible. I could touch my father, his rough beard, the window of the house, the sky visible from the window, the *bukhari* and the *kangri*. Now, in this changing world, all those old things are slipping away from my hands. Along with the things that are being lost, I feel I am also losing a bit of myself. All the new things I touch nowadays come with their dust of separateness. No matter how much I dust them away, I find belongingness only in those old things. But when I sit down to write about them, I can't believe that these things were part of this lifetime.

Then the question arises: What am I actually living? And how true is what I am writing?

In that sense, nothing in this book is true. It is an imaginary world in which a writer sees himself travel—in which the main journey is inwards, of a traveller who is struggling to collect the lived portraits of his childhood. In this entire struggle I have tried to ensure that whoever I met, I left behind a smile on their faces. This is an attempt to share the love that one person shares with another without a relationship.

If this book is in your hands, I hope the fragrance of Kashmir will reach you too.

Manav Kaul

I keep looking in the direction
From where your fragrance wafts in
From where your taste
Takes me to the front of a blue door and white walls

These cracked walls
With their crumbling doors
Make my home
This taste and this smell
Which bring me to the doorstep
That is Kashmir, my home
Whenever I smell Kashmir
My breath begins to bounce off rough, uneven squares
And I see my childhood tiptoeing
Out, across the doorstep

A home never leaves its doorstep
When I had left home
I also couldn't leave
That whole blue sky and all the white clouds
Had come along with me

When someone asks where I live
My response is
I don't live in my home
I roam everywhere with it within me

There were mountains up ahead that weren't visible; the entire city was submerged in rain and fog. When I walked into my room the moisture would cling to my feet, again and again. If I touched my body, I could feel the moistness there as well. I didn't know since when, but my body was adamant about setting out, about going somewhere. Instead of loitering about in one's home, one's emptiness finds more purpose if one wanders around in a strange place. I was always among those who looked for a purpose. Now I had the reason to not do anything. I was in Cherrapunji, and Meghalaya was under lockdown. I couldn't step out, and it was difficult to roam even in the premises of this hotel as the rains would cease only briefly. So, all in all, there was just a room, or one could sit in the dining area. Now that I couldn't step out, the fog would keep roaming with me in my room, in sympathy. I sat at one spot for a long time and watched the passage of time. What is time? If I have paused for now, why does *it* keep flowing so fast? This, and more questions like this perplex me. According to Einstein, time is not the same everywhere. For instance, for the person living in the hills, time runs faster, and for the one living closer to the sea, time is slower. Likewise, for someone static in one place time runs fast, whereas for someone on the move, time seems to move slowly.

For many years I have lived close to the sea, and for a long time I have been roaming about as well. For me, time has always been slow. I often touch the mountains, where time runs faster, and I return. Sitting on the mountains of Cherrapunji I wondered, do they know that time is running fast for them?

I remember once Rooh had asked me, 'If you like the hills so much, why don't you live there?'

I wanted to say yes immediately, but the 'yes' got stuck in my throat. I said, 'I have often thought about this, but I haven't been able to decide.'

'You must first decide if you can exist within what is extremely dear to you.'

Rooh knew my answer. But I had no idea about it. A year earlier, I had decided to buy some land in the hills. I had reached Dehradun with the help of my friends and started scouting. I had taken a book along with me: *Flights* by Olga Tokarczuk. It's a book about travel, in which Olga records her journey as it unfolds. The closer I got to buying land the farther away this book took me from my land. Once I finished this book, I realized that I am not that person who would make a house in the hills and live there. I cannot exist in spaces I love. I want to merely wander in them. Even after so many journeys of my own, I was very far from the kind of journeys recorded in this book. At last, I took a room in Landour and began to work on a novel. I am still carrying the incompleteness of that novel within me.

With the desire of seeing the new mountains, I stayed on in Cherrapunji. There was the Seven Sisters Waterfall in front of me and in the distance was Bangladesh. Few things were visible due to the fog, but seeing less gives you much more than seeing more. This constant moistness, and seeing less as opposed to more, was keeping me in a beautiful dreamlike state. For hours on end I would sit in front of a laptop, correcting my bad writing. I could stay in this state for months. Just then, in this frozen, beautiful set-up of mine, I had a dream. When the dream ended, I saw a bright light entering the room from the balcony. I looked at the time, it was ten already. Truly, time had moved faster in the hills. The clouds were dense, but the rain had held. The imprint of the night could be seen on the morning. I got up but did not immediately sit in front of the laptop; instead, I stepped out on a quest for tea.

After walking for a while, I found a small shop. As soon as the tea touched my hands, I saw the fog enter the shop. Maybe I was still in the dream. I felt that the moment I stepped out of this shop I would be in Kashmir. I had dreamt about Kashmir the previous night. A sudden occurrence of that dream after so many days seemed strange to me. Like the time I had received the news of my father's demise, I had come out of my kitchen and begun pacing in the room outside. I was waiting to stumble. I felt that I was still asleep, and I would wake up immediately as I stumbled. But I didn't and hence couldn't wake up.

When we go far away, a kind of wait begins. We are looking for something that we can't find in the place we had been living in. We have to leave our homes to touch the old roots on which this tree stands. We are not trees, though; we can wander.

When Kashmir had been left behind, I would go back there in my dreams each night. In those dreams, I would take all my recently made friends along too. But when I woke up in the morning, I would find myself crying. Our colony in Khwaja Bagh, Baramulla, was deep within me. Mother would ask, 'Why do you cry every morning when you wake up?' I would lie to her and say, 'Nightmares.' Father was Kashmiri. Whenever I would go to him to talk about my nightmares, I would end up blurting out only one question, 'When will we go back to Kashmir?'

His response to my question was always silence. Later, everyone started scolding me for asking this question. In my struggle to be a good son, I would bury, inside of me, all the thoughts that troubled others. I had banned the mention of our colony in Khwaja Bagh, Baramulla, from all conversations; hence it would often slip into the secret chambers of my dreams, where I had no control over them. Gradually, I began to cry less in the mornings. The dreams of Kashmir, too, became less frequent. Things begin to lose their intensity with time. Now, the dreams of Kashmir make me feel as if an old friend has come to meet me—you feel good when you see them, but you don't know what to do with them.

I was watching the hills of Cherrapunji and thinking about the mountain that was visible from our home in Khwaja Bagh. Then I

asked myself the same question: When will I go to Kashmir? Why
don't I go to Kashmir? Why do I keep roaming in the mountains
that look like Kashmir? I let these questions pass through me as they
appeared. I had no answers for them. All my instruments that I had
used to tackle these questions were rusted.

When we had started living in Hoshangabad, even then, for a
while, we had believed that everything would be normal again and we
would eventually return to Kashmir, and that this was just a delightful
halt. But the conditions in Kashmir kept worsening, and our pit stop
gradually turned into a destination.

We brothers were very young, so any change was like a new
game for us. Just that in this new game, we were two Kashmiri kids.
We wanted to mingle with our new friends, but we looked different.
As soon as we arrived, all the other kids would stop playing and
start staring at us. They would often laugh at how we spoke, because
we weren't able to differentiate between the short 'e' and the long
'e' in Hindi, which remains an issue to date in my writing. I always
kept trying to make our new friends accept us—I stopped bathing;
wherever I saw dirt, dust and mud, I would leap at it. The day I would
bathe and look clean, I would not meet my friends. I wanted to be
invisible in that village, but I had discovered that it was a difficult
task. Initially, it was important to bury Kashmir, so that my mother
and father didn't feel any trouble, but now the reasons had become
even bigger. Now, instead of burying Kashmir inside me I had begun
to trample it.

Suppressing
Trampling
Forgetting
Invisible
Outcry
Accepting
Abandoning
Remembering
Losing
Living with eyes closed
Staring with eyes open

I can still recall each and every lane of Khwaja Bagh. There are a few old names that still bring a smile to my face—Kaka, Baby Aunty, Gagandeep, Titli . . . I still remember how my brother and I would hover around Titli.

Sitting in the dining hall of my hotel in Cherrapunji, I laughed, thinking about Titli. A waiter saw me. Due to the lockdown, I was the only tourist in Cherrapunji, and I had become good friends with the entire staff. He asked me why I was laughing. I just shrugged in response. Some answers are so long that it is better to let them go with just a shrug or shake of the head. Then he asked where I was from. I told him I was from Mumbai. I am still burying Kashmir. But if I say Kashmir, the reply again becomes elaborate. At least the conversation ends when you say Mumbai. When the waiter was turning to go back, I said I was actually from Kashmir. He stopped, and a smile spread across his face. I felt that perhaps hiding Kashmir is nobody else's issue but mine. I returned to my room, and for a long time I kept thinking about the dream.

Dream
I enter from the big gate of Dipper Dredge Colony. Kaka, Suresh, Gagandeep, Titli are all playing but none is looking at me. I go closer to them, but they are all engrossed in themselves. The apple tree near the ground has dried up. Baby Aunty is sitting near that tree. I go closer to her, but she hides. I wanted to go home, but I was constantly missing the turn into my lane. When I finally enter the lane, I don't reach its end. Our home was at the end of the lane, its door was blue and walls were white. I was able to hear the noises coming from there, but I wasn't able to reach them.

About six years ago, when my father was still alive, I had gone to Kashmir—after a gap of about twenty-seven or twenty-eight years. At that time, Rooh was with me. I had gone straight to Srinagar, and called and told my father that I was in Kashmir. I thought he would be happy, but he was quiet at the other end of the line.

I was in class seven when I had gone to Kashmir for the last time with my father. When I saw him talking to his friends, to the car owners in the bazaar, I wasn't able to recognize that this man was my father. He would mingle so well with them, the same way I wanted to mingle with my friends in Hoshangabad. There would be a cheer in his voice, energy and enthusiasm visibly rushing through his body. I would hold on to his finger for dear life, as if I would lose him if I lost my grip. At that time, I felt like telling my father, 'Why don't you stay back here? We have settled into the new place somewhat, but you belong here, to this place.'

During the harsh summers of Madhya Pradesh whenever I would see him getting ice from the fridge rubbed on his skin, I would feel angry at myself for not having told him to stay back when we were in Kashmir.

Father was born in Rainawari in Kashmir. At the age of nineteen he ran away from home and came to Bombay. He worked for a while in the merchant navy in Bombay. Then he began to work in a company that owned cargo ships. He learnt how to navigate a ship, and he travelled the world. After marriage he became an engineer in the dipper dredge department in Baramulla.

There was news of a minor blast in Shillong. The atmosphere became glum. Later, news arrived that a terrorist had also been killed by the army and that there was a curfew in Shillong. Suddenly, these North-east hills began to seem like Kashmir. A strange anxiety seeped into me. I tried sitting down and writing my novel, but I could not write anything. So I left my trip midway and returned to Mumbai.

I had assumed that once I crept back into the bed of my self-created busyness, everything would be all right. Everything was fine on the surface, but my novel had stopped. I was unable to sit peacefully anywhere for long. If I sat with friends, I felt I had to go somewhere; if I got up to leave for home, I realized I was dragging my feet. When I reached home, I felt I had just left from there, and I would remain standing for a long while at the doorstep. I would sit in front of the TV for hours without watching anything. Again and again, I would feel I had to do something, I had to meet someone, but I wasn't able to remember anything accurately. Had my father been alive, I would have called him and asked, 'When shall we return to Kashmir?' I opened my laptop and began to look for tickets from Mumbai to Srinagar. I wanted to book a ticket immediately; I had money, and I had the time. Travelling was the main purpose of my life. The moment I was about to book, I hesitated. What would I do there? This time, I couldn't even call my father from there, saying, 'See, I am in Kashmir.' Why do I want to go to Kashmir? I had no answer for this. I could not book a ticket, and I closed the laptop.

That left over Kashmir
That had felt like it had gone along with my father.
But all that goes away, must find a place somewhere!

Sometimes, somewhere, when I come across of picture of my father,
Something starts throbbing inside of me.
What is it that I am looking at?
Who am I looking at?
I wonder sometimes: Is this my father I'm looking at?
Or is it Kashmir?
Because the fragrance that came from both of them used to be
the same.

Sometimes I saw the peaks of Baramulla on his forehead.
And at other times . . .
I saw the wrinkles of his face
On the chinar leaves

Now, sometimes, this yellowed, torn, aged picture seems like
my Kashmir
And sometimes like the remaining scraps of my father

Does everything we lose
get collected somewhere?

In such moments I often look up at the sky.
There, in some precious moments
I can see the free flow of the Jhelum,
And sometimes I can see my father's smiling face in a soaring eagle,
Free, uninhibited.

Sometimes, something one has written in the past gets heavier in the present. I was insistently going to all those places where I could possibly find an answer to: What would I do there? I hoped for some semblance of movement in that old, yellowed photograph. The past is dead—I kept telling everyone this. I deleted what I had written before and sat again with my novel. This is the story of a class-six boy, and all signs of Kashmir are missing from it. I wanted to drown in this novel. I wanted to create some kind of a new past for myself that had not begun in Kashmir. Can writing save us? I had said this somewhere, and now my own words were beginning to annoy me. Just like time changes and is not the same everywhere, similarly your beliefs also change with place. Something said at a given point of time seems like the absolute truth in that moment, but in another moment, it might have lost its grip on the truth. Time, in fact, doesn't exist, and there is nothing called the truth.

For some days I had taken refuge in my novel. I would push aside any thought remotely connected with Kashmir. I was bothered as to why I was using my own writing to hide from my thoughts. But why not? Couldn't I use my writing as a shield? I went through my writing of the past few days and realized how weak its shield was. I was writing things that weren't related to the novel at all. This novel was close to completion, yet I had started writing a new story from there. I had still not developed the skills to be able to use my writing without revealing myself. I procrastinated writing the ending for long. Now I had nowhere to hide.

I was surprised that a lot of numbers on my phone had been saved with the suffix 'Kashmir'. I don't know since when I had been hoarding these as if in preparation for something. But preparation for what? After scrolling through a lot of them I paused on one:

Shabeer. One of my friends had once given me his number, saying that if I ever went to Kashmir I must call him.

I called. After a few rings, I heard a voice from the other end . . .

'*Salam walekum . . .*'

I didn't respond immediately.

Shabeer asked, '*Ji, janaab*, who is calling?'

'Shabeer Bhai, it is me . . .'

I introduced myself. He knew me a little because of my friends. The moment I told him my full name, he began to talk to me in Kashmiri.

'*Me chhu na Koshur tagan.*' It means, I don't know Kashmiri.

'Why not?' He asked this, too, in Kashmiri, and I don't know how I understood exactly what he was asking. I blurted out a few sentences of apology, and he began to talk to me in Hindi.

He asked, 'So when are you coming?'

'Soon. I just thought I should ask you first if everything is fine there.'

'How can you say something like this about Kashmir? You are a Kashmiri! Of course, everything is fine here.'

'Okay, so when I book my tickets I shall inform you.'

'Ji, janaab,' he said and disconnected the call.

When we lived in Baramulla we used to speak in Kashmiri. There we only spoke to our mother in Hindi. Kashmiri was omnipresent— in school, in bazaars and while playing with our friends. How can one lose a language? Was this the outcome of being plucked from one's native place and being thrown away into a new place, or was it the price I paid for getting assimilated into that new place? I spent my entire childhood hiding my 'Kashmiriyat', but I didn't realize I lost my language in the process. I didn't even know when exactly I had lost the language. Why didn't our father speak to us in Kashmiri? I could never ask him this. Was he frightened at the thought of my going alone to Kashmir? I would never know.

Childhood is never as simple as it seems. In the process of growing up, the corpses of the compromises of childhood show up in the lines that get traced on our faces in those years. I just don't want to hide those dead bodies. Neither do I want to carry those corpses around. I just want to take them to Kashmir and bury them there—where they belong, where I actually belong as well. I wanted to go to Khwaja Bagh Baramulla to bury that childhood of mine that I could no longer live with. I opened my laptop and booked a flight for the fifth.

'I am going to Kashmir,' I said this to myself as if I was saying it to my father.

Sometimes, father would take a long bath, wear a new kurta and take out his yellow diary from the cupboard—we all understood then that now he was going to call his Kashmiri friend Gul Mohammed. It would sometimes happen on the occasion of Shivratri, sometimes on Eid and sometimes on the first day of snow in Kashmir. He would talk sitting in his bed, and their conversation in Kashmiri was so loud that it probably made people on the road imagine that there was a fight taking place inside. But then their intermittent laughter would also be audible. In those moments, a corner of our home would become Kashmir. He needed a lot of tea during this time, even though his body would be drenched in sweat. He had an almirah, the keys to which were always tied to his waist. Occasionally, when he opened the almirah, numerous yellow documents found their way out—government documents, non-government documents, personal documents, numerous letters written in Urdu, several tiny slips with words engraved on them in English and Urdu. He would carefully rearrange all these documents and put them back in his locker. Once, he said, 'When everything shall be all right again, all these documents shall come in handy. I would go by myself and show them everything.'

I wanted to ask, 'To whom?' but my urge fell short in front of his enthusiasm. I always felt he was waiting for some Judgement Day. One fine day, someone, god knows who, might ask him what evidence you have to prove that you are a Kashmiri, and all these documents would then be useful. Our father had kept these documents away from us. This was something only he could do.

As soon as I booked that ticket to Kashmir it felt as if a new doorway had opened. I could now see things better but not so much as to be able to claim that I am a Kashmiri. Even today, when I introduce myself, I take my time in saying that I was born in Kashmir. This is, however, not deliberate. It is just like the fact that I don't mention readily that I am also a writer. Because after saying this the questions that follow are often so inane that I regret having mentioned that I am a writer. For instance, people ask me: So, what do you write about? Have you ever been heartbroken? Why do you travel alone? Is your grief the reason for your writing? Why don't you write films? I have a story; will you write it for me? Can you please narrate something? Do you have any motivational books? It is a long list.

Each writer is unique and so the relationship with their writing is also unique to each. Similarly, each person born in Kashmir has a distinct relationship with Kashmir. My father's Kashmir is definitely not my Kashmir.

Leaving Kashmir and coming to Madhya Pradesh in my childhood was an interesting event for me. I was excited about my new home, new friends and the new school. However, for my father this event was a minor pause and a cause for prolonged pain. He did not even throw away his warm clothes for a long while. He firmly believed that we would return. One day, when I was transitioning to college from school, I came to know that my father had thrown away all his warm clothes. He had not mentioned it to anyone. He never took his Kashmir out of his Godrej almirah. The enormity of what he had done became clearer as time passed. He had stopped stepping out of the house. Other than urgent stuff at the bank, etc., he never left the house. Later, he stopped leaving his bed as well. He had surrendered in a way. I was young and, instead of understanding these changes in him, would argue with him, and each argument degenerated into a strange fight. I wanted him to go for a walk every day, do some yoga and take care of himself. He always had some excuse or the other—it is very hot; I shall begin after the rains; when it is less cold; first I shall buy a good pair of shoes and a tracksuit and then I shall do all of this every day.

The impact of being separated from one's own land gradually creeps into all that you have lived through. We cannot pinpoint one moment and say conclusively: This was the impact of leaving Kashmir. I could never fathom that impact even while living with my father. I didn't have even the faintest idea. These facts revealed themselves after his demise. While he was alive, he never let his Kashmir fall off his bed.

On his father's back he used to draw
His own future with his nails

His father had the skin of a mountain dweller.
But just for him, he used to keep his skin rough and uneven.
Lest he ever find it difficult to outline his future.

One day, he stopped in the middle of his artwork.
'What happened, son?' asked the father.
He replied, 'It's done!'
And his father got up and left.

The American Army was leaving Afghanistan, and Taliban had taken control. Its impact was evident in Kashmir as well. One of my friends said that the situation had got worse in Kashmir and I should delay my trip. I had booked my tickets. Just then, with the death of the separatist leader Geelani, the situation had become even more sensitive. I tried to contact Shabeer, but his phone wasn't reachable. I came to know that phone and Internet services had been suspended in Kashmir for a few days. I thought about listening to my friend's advice. Then I realized that I was not going to either Shimla or Manali; this was Kashmir—always on fire due to all of its political, religious, economic, social and communal issues.

The images of Kashmir that I had collected in my childhood were entirely different from what Kashmir was now and as it appeared in the news. I still watch the news as if they are talking about some other place also known as Kashmir. Even today, to me Kashmir means a blue door and white walls, and the antics of snowy white clouds in a deep blue sky.

Apples, bukhari, kangri, *kulcha*, snow and mountains and smiling faces . . .

I could never ask my father what faces of Kashmir he remembered. Could he see the blue door and white walls in his images of Kashmir? Just like time is different in different places, similarly the past is also different for each. All of us had collected distinct images of the times when we lived together in Khwaja Bagh, Baramulla. If a particular day was mentioned to each one of us, even then we would have different stories of the same day. Maybe in my stories the day we left Kashmir would not be so significant, but for my father there could be no other day as important as that one. The displacement from Kashmir was deeply experienced by my father, but I cannot feel it in the same way.

When pasts are so distinct, all the presents too have their own distinct expanses; it is difficult to be certain which memory would bring a smile to which face.

Therefore, if you have picked up this book to understand the political, religious, economic, social and communal situation of Kashmir, you will be disappointed. I don't know why I am writing this book. I don't even know whether this writing will finally take the shape of a book. I just want to touch those images again that I had gathered in my childhood. Maybe that's why even in the current situation in Kashmir I wasn't reluctant to go there. I don't know what might happen in the future at all.

In Baramulla, Khwaja Bagh, Titli lived right above our house. My brother, Titli and I . . . we played together all the time—all the games, games in the middle of a game, and our tired laughter after the games were exactly the same. My brother and I were not as sad to leave Kashmir as we were about getting separated from Titli. She was our first love. We could never find out whom she loved more between us. I knew precisely what was making me cry while leaving Khwaja Bagh, but I didn't want to appear weak in front of Titli, and so I held myself together. While leaving, my brother had asked Titli for her photograph. I was surprised when my brother did this. Everything between us had always been divided into three. For the first time my brother had asked for something from Titli that was entirely his, and I had no claim on it. I was sure that Titli would refuse, but she took out a picture from her schoolbag and gave it to him. I kept thinking for a long time—I should have also asked for a memento or given her something for memory's sake. But what could I have asked for and what could I have given? We left Baramulla for Srinagar.

This happened years ago. Now we had become two fair-skinned boys of a small district of Madhya Pradesh who didn't like talking to each other much. Kashmir was in our stories still, but whenever there was mention of Kashmir, we could see Titli flying away. I had noticed that every time Kashmir was mentioned, my brother would immediately go to the other room. I was aware that in the other room, he would be staring at that black-and-white picture of Titli. Outside, I would be regretting the fact that I didn't even cry in front of her. I had to really please my brother, run several errands for him, and then, on some afternoons, he would let me look at Titli. The only condition was I could not touch the picture, and staring was prohibited. Most probably, it was a photograph taken out from her school ID. She looked like a fairy in the photo—one who could step out any time and say, 'Let's fly!'

That picture didn't stay for long in the pockets of my brother's shorts. We had also begun to grow up, wandering in the bylanes of that village. Titli flew away from our lives gradually.

When Father was on his last trip to Kashmir some years ago, he had met Titli's family on his way back to Jammu. He told us this, and we both blurted out together, 'How is Titli?' Father told us, 'She was married off. During the delivery of her first baby her legs became paralysed. Her husband abandoned her. She passed away sometime ago due to depression.'

After speaking about Titli in brief sentences between sips of tea, Father got back to narrating his anecdotes about meeting Baby Aunty. But neither of us wanted to know about anyone else. After a long silence my brother got up and went inside. Now he didn't even have the picture. What would Bhai be doing inside? For a long time I stood quietly outside his room. Then I took out the torn and faded black-and-white photograph of Titli from my mathematics notebook. I had stolen the photo long ago from my brother's pocket. I wanted to go to Bhai's room and give the picture to him that very moment, but it was risky. So, I went to the courtyard and buried the picture under a broken wall.

I don't know how many years ago I wrote about this incident. Now, in my preparation to return to Kashmir, all of this was coming back to me. How much of Kashmir lay scattered in my writings? In all my poems, where I mention a cloud, the cloud belongs to nowhere else but Khwaja Bagh. Every character that I have named Titli is the one whose picture I had buried under the broken wall of my home back then. Every time I say 'tea', the four o'clock tea made by my mother in Khwaja Bagh is what I remember. In the fragrance of home, a large part is Kashmir. Can all of this be buried?

On the way to the airport I was breathing hard. I felt a strange anxiety. Was this the right time to go to Kashmir? The question came up repeatedly, like an ache. But when is the right time? Time is imaginary. It takes the shape of how you live in it. I was at the airport and was heading towards gate 45A, holding a coffee in my hand.

A day before I'd tried to call Shabeer, and the phone had started ringing. As soon as he picked up, he began to speak in Kashmiri. I understood that there was no use interrupting him. I could only assume and guess what he was saying, and, accordingly, keep answering in Hindi. Towards the end I asked him for the address; he said something in Kashmiri that probably meant he would come to pick me up.

'Where would you come to pick me up? At the airport?' I asked.

He said, 'No, in Anantnag.'

'But where in Anantnag?'

'You don't worry. I will meet you there,' he said.

I couldn't understand anything. So, I said in the end, '*Dost*, if the phone stops working, how will I find you?'

'Why do you worry? I will find you.'

I said, 'Fine!' and disconnected the call. I didn't understand why going to Anantnag had to be under this blanket of secrecy.

Sitting on the plane, I looked at the faces of all the passengers. They were all going to Srinagar—I don't know why I was happy about this.

The last time I had landed at the Srinagar airport, Rooh was with me . . .

As soon as we had stepped out of the airport, I'd stopped.

Rooh had asked me, 'What happened?'

I'd said, 'I know this fragrance.'

'What fragrance?'

'This fragrance, of the valley, my Kashmir, it is still the same.'

I kept taking in long breaths this time too, but that fragrance was missing. I had a strange thought—maybe it was because the last time my father was around and this time he was not. Whom did the fragrance belong to? Kashmir or my father? The Internet was shut, but the phone was working. I called Shabeer, and he said that he was waiting for me. *Somebody was waiting for me in Kashmir . . .* These words brought out bitter-sweet emotions. By the time I could convert this emotion into a smile the emotion was gone. The taxi owner was eating lavasa, Kashmiri bread, with tea. I asked for a piece of that bread and put it in my mouth. Last time around, the fragrance of Kashmir had come to me as soon as I'd landed at the airport; this time its taste was on my tongue.

There was a crossing at some distance from the airport; to the left was Baramulla and to the right, Anantnag. I was desperate to see the blue door and the white walls, but now I was headed in the opposite direction. I was reminded of my dream where I was in my colony in Khwaja Bagh, Baramulla, but was unable to get home.

'Is everything all right in Baramulla?' I asked the taxi driver, masking my fears.

'Yes, everything is fine, don't worry.'

Maybe I should have asked: 'Is everything all right in Kashmir?' And then asked about Baramulla. My fears were still unattended to, but he had given his reply.

Shabeer had opened a restaurant ahead of Anantnag, so we went straight there. I recognized Shabeer the moment I looked at him. I felt I could recognize Shabeer even in a crowd in Delhi. Kashmiri faces are evident from a distance. The entire day he kept asking about my plans, and I could utter just two names: Khwaja Bagh and Rainawari, Srinagar. I wanted to go there the very next day. He said these could be covered in two days. What next? I have never had any answers for 'what next'. I wanted to say to him that these trips would not be over in just two days. Each place would drop like a pebble into the silent lake inside me, and the ripples will spread for days. I kept looking at the mountains of Pahalgam behind his restaurant for a long while.

I was not a Kashmiri. I felt I had come to pick up the tattered pieces of my lost Kashmiriyat in front of Shabeer, who was a full-fledged Kashmiri. When I spoke about Kashmir in Mumbai, I felt it was my right, because I was a Kashmiri. But here, the voice, that sense of entitlement, had weakened. Who am I fooling? I am not a Kashmiri. I had nothing except the images I had gathered in

21

my childhood. I thought I should tell the Titli story to Shabeer, but then I began to feel shy about it.

Shabeer asked, 'Do you want to go to Pahalgam?'

I just shrugged. Shabeer had called his friend Mushtaq. We came out of the restaurant where Mushtaq stood next to his extremely old Maruti.

'So, I should go to Pahalgam now?' I had asked Shabeer, but, in fact, I wanted to ask myself this question. Shabeer, too, shrugged in reply.

In a while Mushtaq and I were on our way to Pahalgam. Mushtaq had been quiet in front of Shabeer, but now he was extremely chatty. For a long time he tried taking me to all the touristy places of Pahalgam, but the moment I saw a crowd I would ask him to reverse the car.

He asked, irritated, 'Arré! Then where do you want to go?'

I pointed at a roadside bakery. 'Let's go there and have *girda** and kahwa.'

'Arré, let's go further, janaab. There is much to be seen in Pahalgam.'

Mushtaq took a long time to understand that I hadn't actually wanted to come to Pahalgam. When we moved forward after having girda and kahwa, I saw a dense deodar forest beside the road. I asked him to park on the side, and we entered the forest.

'There are many such places in Kashmir,' Mushtaq said as he sat on the grassy ground.

'These places are so special.'

I could lay bare my Kashmir in front of Mushtaq. There was something about him that put one at ease. I kept touching and looking at the deodar trees. How nice it was to roam with this form of life, hundreds of years old; what all they might have witnessed, and, in spite all that, they stood quietly, emanating so much peace and calm. I lay down under a tree. Mushtaq walked down to the river, washed his hands and sat down at a distance to perform the namaz. There could not be a more pious place than this to pray.

---

* Kashmiri bread.

Later that night we returned to Anantnag. I stayed at Shabeer's house. When I came down after freshening up, Shabeer took me straight to the kitchen. A *dastarkhwan* had been set up there, and his entire family was waiting around it to have a meal with me. My gaze travelled first to his father—his face, his body, the way he was sitting, the manner in which he spoke made him seem so similar to my father. I made space and sat next to him. Sitting there in his white kurta pajama, he would glance at me again and again. I had a strong desire to smell him—I was sure that I would get the same fragrance from him that I had sensed when I had landed in Kashmir six years ago. In the hope of catching that fragrance again I stayed next to him, but I couldn't muster up the courage to smell him. He would think that I was mad! The meal consisted of *nadru*, meat, rice and *haak*.* I ate a lot, as if I had been hungry for many years. When I returned to my room my eyes were bloodshot. Shabeer looked at me and said, 'You seem to be sleepy. You must sleep.'

'I have to write,' I said.

I took out my laptop, and my fingers began to dance on the keyboard. I wish I knew how to write! I wish I knew how to live! The gap between the movement of my fingers and what I was feeling so intensely in that moment was so huge that I could see the knots in the formation of each sentence being written. Then, in the process of untying the knots, I would get so entangled that I would lose my grip on what exactly I was feeling. There was a tiff going on between my living and my being. I would write and delete, again write and again delete. Each time I felt I was being untruthful. Every time the word 'Kashmir' would appear in front of my eyes, I wondered why this word seemed to be so distant. I left my Kashmir. I tried to write Shabeer's Kashmir or tried to narrate from Mushtaq's point of view. Why had my Kashmir faded so much? I felt a guilt about how I was trying to write 'Kashmir' sitting amid people who were actually

---

* Nadru: lotus stems; haak: collard greens.

Kashmiri. But am I writing 'Kashmir'? Absolutely not. I took a deep breath and began to write what I had once seen, smelt and tasted.

In the morning Shabeer and I went towards the river behind the house. In the distance, someone was sweeping a floor, cocks were crowing, and other than the chirping of the sparrows the entire village was still asleep.

I said to Shabeer as we were walking, 'I woke up to the sound of the azan, and then more sounds of the azan began filtering in from all over, it sounded like an orchestra of azans.'

He said embarrassedly, 'Yes, that would happen here. Masjids all around.'

'I like that. I slept again after that.'

'Did you write something at night?' he asked.

My ears always crave to hear such words. 'The brain wanted to write but the body gave up.'

'So, you can sit and write today.'

'I can't write like that. I need a lot of time.'

'There is plenty of time here.'

'No, I need a lot of solitude. Maybe not even solitude, but my writing begins when I am thoroughly bored.'

'So?'

'So, I will have to go somewhere else.'

'Where?'

'Baramulla or Srinagar.'

'When?'

'I will leave after tea.'

'Okay, let's talk.'

We both fell silent. At that moment I was sitting in Shabeer's special place, where he had been sitting since his youth. He told me nothing had changed here, that it was still exactly the same. I know Shabeer wanted to say that I could also come here and write, but he didn't say that. After some time we bought lavas for the entire family from the bakery and sat in the kitchen. Everyone was already in the kitchen having sheer chai. I again sat next to Shabeer's abbu. As soon as I settled, he asked me, 'Do you people not allow anyone to enter the kitchen like this?'

There was an awkward and brief silence in the kitchen after that, maybe because they had heard him speak Hindi after a long time. I told him hurriedly that it was not like that in our home and also in some other homes. Then, thinking deeply and speaking in staccato phrases, I fell silent. Shabeer's father had said 'you people', and in that categorization I had become the spokesperson for all Kashmiri Pandits. I have always been caught in such conversations in Kashmir. What if my father were here now? What would be his reply?

'In the Pandit homes, they don't even enter their own kitchen without bathing.'

Shabeer came to my rescue in that conversation. Then they all began to converse in Kashmiri, and I felt a lot of fingers being pointed at me during that entire chitchat. The word 'Islamabad' was also mentioned several times. When everyone became silent, I asked, 'Do you people have some connection with Islamabad?'

Everyone laughed. I was served sheer chai, and I began to eat lavas with it by breaking it into small pieces. When we used to live in Srinagar, getting lavas every morning was my duty. I used to bring warm lavas straight from the oven at the bakery. Ma would have made tea by then, and my father, wearing his pheran, would wait for the lavas.

'The name Anantnag is used for official purposes only, but all Kashmiris call it Islamabad. Like my name is Gul Mohammed. All the people in the family and the village call me Gul, but for people outside I am Shabeer. Everyone laughed because you asked this just like an outsider would.'

I was embarrassed. I had nothing more to say after that. I was actually an outsider, although Shabeer and his family were so affectionate that with them I felt as if I was one of them. Gul Mohammed was my father's friend, with whom he chatted for hours on the phone. I had seen these words written in big bold letters in his small yellow diary: Gul Mohammed. I had thought that I would tell Shabeer about my father's friend, but in my preparation to go to Srinagar I didn't think it held much importance. I often fail to mention such small details, and after giving appropriate details, I often look back and think that even if that wasn't said it wouldn't have made much of a difference.

Mushtaq readied the car, and I packed my stuff. When we were putting the stuff in the car, we saw that Shabeer's father was also ready to come along.

'Where are you going?' Shabeer asked jokingly.

'With my other son,' he answered.

He was talking about me. I looked lovingly at him. He was wearing a cap with the slogan 'Born Free'. Shabeer and I sat in the back and he in the front.

'Your cap seems to be too tight. Let me loosen it up a bit.'

He took off his cap and gave it to Shabeer, and Shabeer wore it in order to get a sense of the size and then loosened it up a little. 'Hmm . . .' is all he said when he wore it back, acknowledging that it was fine now. I was envious of the relationship Shabeer and his father shared. We dropped Shabeer and his abbu at the J&K Bank ATM. I wanted to come out and hug him, but by then he had extended his hand. After shaking his hand, I hugged Shabeer and watched them leave.

My father had not been able to leave Kashmir for a long time because of Gul Mohammad. When the tensions has escalated, Gul Mohammad had said, 'Jigra, you become Muslim, and I will become a Hindu, then let's see who has the courage to throw us out.' Still, my father had to leave. But their friendship remained just as strong.

There was news that there could be a curfew in Srinagar. Mushtaq called his friends in Srinagar to ask about the situation. Mushtaq was more scared than I was.

'I rarely go to Srinagar. There is always a huge risk of getting stuck there,' he said as he sat in the car.

'We'll see what happens.'

I wasn't too scared now, and I couldn't understand Mushtaq's fears. Time and again a few army vehicles would cross us;

Mushtaq would give them way each time and pull his car to the side. The weather was beautiful, and the villages through which the road passed before hitting the highway gave me glimpses of Kashmiri life.

'Right now, you and I are nobodies, so we needn't be afraid. We don't count for anything. Neither do we have an agenda. We don't want to do anything, good or bad. We are simply living our lives without any changes. So we are nobody. We don't have to fear anyone. But if one gets caught in a crossfire, then that's a different matter altogether.'

'Have you ever been caught in a crossfire?'

'When I was in the tenth standard, I loved a girl madly. One day, while returning from school, I stopped her. She didn't want to speak to me, and I didn't have the courage to say anything to her. I kept looking at her. We were on one side of the road, and the way to my home was from the other side of the road. After a while she asked, "What is it?" I panicked and began to run towards the other side of the road. She called out my name, "Mushtaq," and I stopped in the middle of the road. Right then, there was a blast on the other side of the road. Had she not stopped me, I would have been in the middle of that blast. She saved my life.'

'What happened to that girl?'

'You don't care that I am alive?'

'Now, I am an ordinary person. That which we cannot see is definitely more interesting,' I said, almost whining.

'Yes, you are a writer, so you are more interested in her.'

I smiled and he kept driving quietly.

'Will you have tea?'

'Yes, let's stop somewhere.'

We came to a small shop by the roadside. Mushtaq was hungry as well. He ordered noon chai and roti, and I ordered kahwa.

'This is Pulwama. You see the other side of the road? That's where the bus blast happened. The next day I was crossing the same road. The shutters of the shops had burst open. There was a crowd of news reporters.'

'Weren't you scared to cross this place the next day?'

'Everyone around here has got used to it. Even when bullets are being fired on one side of the road, people go on doing their routine jobs on the other side. It's a different matter that the Pulwama blast was huge, but I had to go home also.'

When we started towards Srinagar after the tea halt, I was again thinking about that girl. I couldn't stop myself and asked, 'Are you married?'

I wanted to bring the discussion back to that girl, but had I asked directly, Mushtaq would have been irritated.

'No, sir. I haven't been able to get out of my one-sided love for the girl who had saved my life as yet.'

After saying this he started playing old Rafi songs. Maybe this was what I too was waiting for.

'Have you decided where you would stay in Srinagar?'

'We shall first go to Rainawari, and then I will decide.'

I was trying to dodge the question. I just knew that I didn't want to stop at Nigeen Lake. Six years ago, that was where I had stayed with Rooh, and I didn't want to relive those days by going back there. In any case, there was so much to relive.

When we are rushing through time it becomes slower. The time inside the car was slow-moving. Whenever Mushtaq would stop the car and ask for directions to Rainawari, I would repeat and save those Kashmiri words inside me. We were eventually approaching Rainawari or Rainvar, where our ancestral house was. My father was born here. We used to come here from Baramulla during festivals.

'They are saying Rainawari is a big place. Where exactly do you want to go?' Mushtaq asked me. The one who was waiting to give us directions was peeping in through the car's window.

'Just Rainawari. When we reach the crossing ahead, maybe I will remember something.'

Mushtaq said something to him in Kashmiri, and we drove further. After some time, we reached the Rainawari crossing. I was looking at the sky. There were kites flying. Whenever I used to sit at the window of our home here, I would keep looking at the kites. These are the kites mentioned in my stories and plays.

'Reached! Now where do we go?'

Mushtaq was sure that I actually didn't remember anything. In a way he was right. All I remembered was the broken wall of a school, and that the lane of our house was ahead of it. I told him, 'Let's turn into this left lane.'

Mushtaq reluctantly turned into that lane. Rainawari had changed a lot. His question was valid. The last I'd stayed there was in 1988. Now, almost all homes were new here and a few old ones were in ruins. In a mental haze, I was struggling to get a sense of recognition from the old images in my head. Just then we turned into a narrow lane, and I saw the wall of the school. It was the same still. Slightly more dilapidated, yet the same. Excitedly, I ask Mushtaq to stop the car.

'Where is the house?'

'Not house, wall . . . the wall of the school. Just stop the car here.'

I jumped out. As I looked into the lane of my house, which had been a short distance from there, I saw that it was a dead end. There was a large house, and its gates were closed; I didn't recognize any of the big houses behind the gate. By that time Mushtaq had parked the car and joined me. I was standing at that one spot—frozen.

'Which house is it?'

'It was here only, but this is all new.'

When we entered the gates, I realized that a house had been constructed in the courtyard of our house. In the garden, where we used to grow vegetables, another house had been constructed. All the old remnants had been buried deep. There were walls on all the four sides, and the entrance now was not from here but from the main road.

We lived in a considerably small house in Hoshangabad—my mother, father, brother and I used to sleep in a row in a room. There was a small kitchen beside that. We had gone there from our spacious home in Rainawari. Financially, too, we were in a bad shape.

Our debts were growing; my father would not get his salary regularly. I was too young then to understand the financial difficulties at home. Some things weren't available to us then. We had been pulled out of a private school and put in a government school. From an English-medium school, we had now been shifted to a Hindi-medium school. My father thought that an early retirement was the solution to these issues. Whatever general provident fund he would get would be enough to pay off some debts and get some cash in hand. But as soon as he took that early retirement his office was attacked and all the papers were burned. Neither did he get any money nor did his pension begin. He had to provide evidence that he worked there. He didn't get any retirement money, but he wanted at least the pension to start coming in.

I saw that he continually wrote letters to numerous people at that time. He started getting a mutable pension, but his permanent pension and GPF were still stuck. He would get angry every now and then, and sit down to write the letters—sometimes to Ghulam Nabi Azad, sometimes to the pension department of the J&K government. But till his death he neither got his full pension nor the GPF money.

Both of us were growing up, but we never had the slightest inclination that we were in debt. Then, one day, Father decided to sell the house in Rainawari. He went to Kashmir and sold the entire house at a minimal price. That money was divided among the three brothers. As far as I remember, each one got about three and a half lakh. That money settled our debts. Due to the debts and the sudden economic depression my father never had any expectations from me or my brother. He stayed away from the conversations about our future. He had stopped stepping out of the new house after selling the Rainawari property. He would go to take his mutable pension from the Jammu and Kashmir Bank and come straight back home. I never heard him mention Rainawari after that.

I walked to the back of the Rainawari house, trying to peek across the wall to spot maybe some patch of the past. Then I saw a very old man peeping at us from a window in the wall of the adjacent house. His home looked quite old. Mushtaq and I approached him, and when Mushtaq explained to him in Kashmiri why I had come there, he gave us a big smile. I folded my hands in namaskar, greeted him and said, 'Our house was here. There was a big courtyard between the two houses.'

'Yes, there was a courtyard and a garden in the front.'

'Yes, now it is all . . .' I couldn't complete my sentence.

'Everything is gone now. Whose son are you?'

'I am Manohar's son.'

'Manohar?'

Then I remembered. 'Makhan Lal.' In Kashmir everyone knows each other by their nicknames.

'O! You are Makhna's son. How is he?' he asked.

'He is no more now.'

'Oh. He died?'

'Did you know him?'

When I asked him this, he began to look at the houses that had cropped up in place of our house. 'The other two?'

'They have also passed away.'

When I said this, he removed his elbows from the windowsill and went inside muttering something. I looked at Mushtaq, trying to make sense of what he was muttering.

'He is calling us inside. Should we go?'

Mushtaq and I were sitting in a small room that had an old carpet. There were torn cushions scattered all around. We couldn't see anyone else, and the old man was inside. He came out in a while with tea.

'It's Lipton tea,' he said, placing the cups down.

We both picked our respective cups.

'You will not have tea?'

'I don't have this tea.'

I don't know why I asked him, 'What is your name?'

'Gul Mohammed.'

I was stunned.

'My father used to call you.'

'No, we've never had a phone at our place.'

After a bit of silence, he said, 'Once a thief had entered your house. Your father woke up and leapt at the thief. The scared thief jumped out of the window. But Makhan Lal was crazy—he jumped out of the window behind the thief. Don't know how far he went, but he caught him and brought him as well as all the stolen stuff back. He used to be short-tempered. Once my *bub** had scolded him, so he left home and never visited again.'

I had many questions for him, but after saying this he got up, went inside and closed the door. Mushtaq and I sat waiting for him for some time. Then Mushtaq bid him farewell loudly in Kashmiri. We got no response from inside.

I said to Mushtaq, 'There was a Shiva temple here close to the Dal. Let's go and check whether it is still there.'

'If you say so, it must be there,' said Mushtaq.

When we were crossing the market close to our house in Rainawari, I was surprised that the shops I remembered were still there. The place from where we bought milk and curd, where we bought meat, the bakery . . . I was looking at the old people sitting in front of these shops. They must've known my father. He would have bargained at these shops. I had walked this market several times holding his tubby finger. I wanted to go to every shop and tell each shopkeeper that Makhan Lal had now passed away. All the old men looked like my father. He was born here, among these people; he had grown up among them. Would I also begin to look like these people in a few years?

---

* Grandfather.

The Shiva temple was there. I went inside, but it was locked. A family that had migrated from Uttar Pradesh looked after it. They opened the gates at my request, and I kept looking at the Shivling inside for hours. My father used to visit this temple a lot; he was a devotee of Lord Shiva. After a while I couldn't bear to stand there any longer. I told Mushtaq, 'Let's go from here.'

'Where?'

I had now reached Nigeen Lake. The more I tried to run away from my past, the more I was drawn towards it. Mushtaq wished to be with me, but I told him that I wanted to get bored and would catch up with him later. When he was going back on a shikara, I asked him, 'So, what happened to that girl?' He smiled and shrugged.

I am truly a writer. I keep chasing the mysterious darkness, looking for stories hidden behind the invisible. The boathouse owner recognized me instantly. I requested him for a cheap room. He suggested that I live where I had stayed the last time. I said no immediately. I told him that I neither wanted that houseboat nor that room. He had three houseboats. They were all lying vacant due to the ongoing tensions. He showed me a small houseboat; its room was ordinary. I liked it. I took it after slight bargaining.

'How many days would you stay for?'

'I have no idea,' I said.

After dumping my stuff in my room in the houseboat I came out. We can never be too far away from where we once lived; it just remains at a left turn or right turn away from us. For a long time, I kept looking at the houseboat on my right. This was just six years ago. I had stayed in that houseboat with Rooh. I couldn't resist it; I turned to my right and stood in front of the last room of that houseboat. The door was shut. The emptiness of the room had extended itself to the other side of the door too, followed by darkness and the wait for the probable stories in the invisible.

'Wait'—I had become wary of this word and the expansive world this word opens, and of myself. Where and how had I become like this? I wanted to leave but my feet froze. They had become used to waiting for stories. I would have to take something from here or my feet would not move. I could smell the fragrance of wood from the boat. It was a fragrance similar to that of Rooh's hair—her soft fingers, her laughter. She used to say, 'I can't laugh so much with anyone as much as I do with you.' I had also always wanted to say the same to her.

Someone was calling out for me. When I came out, the boy who worked at the boat had got kahwa and kulchas for me.

'These would have turned cold, that's why I called out for you,' he said.

'Okay, janaab.'

'Why don't you stay there?'

'This boat is also good, and one should stay at different places.'

'Your wish. That one is also vacant. Whenever you want, I shall put your things there.'

When he was about to go back, I was reminded of his name. 'Basheer Bhai!'

'Ji, janaab.'

'I won't stay there.'

This time I had said that looking straight into his eyes. He also kept looking at me for a while, and then he turned around and went. I think had he stayed back looking at me for longer, I would have asked him to put my stuff there.

Italo Calvino has written somewhere in *Invisible Cities*, 'The city, however, does not tell its past, but contains it like the lines of a hand . . .'

Whatever is commonplace for Shabeer and Mushtaq weighs me down. Every night before I sleep, I take a deep breath and ask myself, 'What am I doing here?' I have changed; Kashmir is also not the same. Since the moment I left Kashmir, we had been running in opposite directions. Now, sometimes a glimpse of the past reveals itself and my eyes light up. Maybe the same Kashmir also sees glimpses of belongingness in me. Now that I am finally sitting down to write, I am not able to either write down 'Kashmir' nor bear the heaviness that is weighing my shoulders down.

Today, the Internet was restored. Gradually things began to normalize, but there were other kinds of news as well. If you talk to anyone here—Basheer Bhai, the baker, the auto driver—they are all filled with bitterness about Kashmiri politics. Their voices bear the weariness of living the same day every day. People gaze at me intently at every question I ask. Maybe they want to understand what exactly I want to know. I have to keep my questions light. I recoil from the politics that has led to the weariness in their voices. The situation in the Valley is all right—What does that mean? I am yet to understand that. But the moment a tourist arrives, they make a bundle of their weariness and push it down the Dal.

Earning a living pushes their worries aside, even if momentarily. They don't see anything tourist-like in me. Solo travellers are neither respected in Europe nor here.

Just now a man passed by carrying some carpets, flowers and handicrafts in his small shikara. Looking at me, he slowed down his rowing. He began to inspect me closely. He was trying to make things out by looking into my eyes. He was trying to find his customer in me. I would take a sneak peek at him while writing about him on my laptop. He had come close to my houseboat. The closer he came, the more the disappointment on his face grew. Finally, I met his gaze and smiled only enough to make him feel better but not enough to seem like a potential customer. My houseboat is at the far end of Nigeen Lake. I understand how far he had to row to reach here. I looked at him again. He was closer now, and a smile formed on my lips. He listed his shikara towards my houseboat. He said namaskar to me after coming on board and sat next to me as if that was what he had come here for.

He asked, 'Has madam also come along?'

'I am alone. I will not buy anything. If you want to have some tea, I can offer that.'

I wanted to keep the details of my being alone a little foggy; that was why I spoke so much.

'Never mind. What do you do?' he asked.

'I am a writer.'

'See, just like you are a writer, I am an artist. When someone reads what you have written, it makes you feel good. Similarly, I have also handcrafted all of this. If you just see it once, I will feel good. Don't buy but just see. You are an artist, you must know the worth of this.'

I had no counterargument for this, so I said yes. He brought two big bags inside. I had decided that I would not buy anything, but finally I did buy a small wooden tortoise.

Her name was Roohi, I called her Rooh. We had first met at a pub in New York. I was going through a phase when I just wanted to be wasted; hence I would remain drunk with some excuse or the other. I had no interest in anything. With my back turned on New York, I sat in the pubs holding my drinks for hours. That night, I'd had more than my usual share. She was with her friends. Whenever I heard a Hindi word in their conversation my eyes would meet hers. I was on my fifth peg. I need four pegs to be wasted. Just then I heard her voice close to me, 'I have seen you somewhere, your face seems familiar.' She had said this in English.

'Faces like mine are called a common Indian face.'

She laughed, extended her hand and introduced herself, and I heard 'Rooh'. She was of a wheatish complexion, with her hair tied up in an unruly bun; she was tall with eloquent eyes. I told her my name, and she looked at me surprised. 'Kashmir. Are you a Kashmiri?'

'Yes.'

> *'I came by the public road*
> *But won't return on it*
> *On the embankment I stand,*
> *Halfway through the journey.*
> *Day is gone. Night has fallen.*
> *I dig in my pockets but can't find a cowry shell.*
> *What can I pay for the ferry?'*

I couldn't understand anything. I kept gazing at her, and she kept looking at me with surprise.

'What is this?'

'You don't know?'

'No.'

'You are a Kashmiri, and you don't know this?'

'Yes, I don't know. So what?' I was beginning to get irritated. I turned away.

'This is Lal Ded.'

I was in such a condition at that time that whatever felt like mine was pushed away by me. By the time I looked back at her she had stood up from her stool.

'I thought you would be happy to hear Lal Ded. Have a good evening.'

She was gone, and I had finished my fifth drink.

Before coming to New York, I had created a circle around me into which nobody would be given an entry. But there was no hope of anyone entering the circle in New York anyway, and hence the walls had developed cracks, and through them Rooh had entered that circle. I staggered up to Rooh. She was sitting with her friends at a corner of the bar.

'Would you like to go out with me, right now? I wanted to talk to you.'

I'd said it all at once and waited for her response. I knew that she would refuse and I would gulp down this insult with another drink.

'Okay, but on one condition.'

'Whatever you say.'

'Sure? You might regret this.'

'Tell me.'

'Would you take me to Kashmir?'

'Right now?' I asked, almost startled.

She began to laugh at this. Her friends also began to laugh with her. I also wanted to laugh but couldn't. Laughing, she picked up her things and was ready to go with me. Her friends were alarmed. 'Are you crazy! Do you even know him?' But without bothering about her friends she stepped out of the bar with me.

'Where should we go?' I asked.

'Kashmir,' she said, and I don't know after how many days I found myself laughing.

T.S. Eliot wrote somewhere, 'Home is where one starts from.'

Nigeen Lake was so calm that it seemed as if there was black glass spread out in front of the boat. I had requested Basheer Bhai to put my food outside. He was standing beside me in the dark.

'How is the haak?'

'Just like home'

'I got it made from home.'

I don't know what to do about these relations. Basheer was so warm six years ago, and even now he had picked up the conversation on same note. I liked haak as much even back then, especially the haak made at his home.

'There is nobody around here. Are you alone here these days?' I asked.

'The situation in Kashmir is not good right now. Hence I have let people go.'

After dinner, I went to the upper half of the houseboat for a stroll. I heard him call out from below, 'Will you have noon chai?'

'Yes, sure.'

I had lit a cigarette and was looking at the houseboat in front of me in which Rooh and I had stayed together the last time around. We would sit on the deck after a meal. I would smoke, and she would read some book written about Kashmir.

'You should have stayed in that boat only,' Basheer said as he handed me the noon chai.

'I was also thinking of the same thing.'

'We can still move there.'

'No, this is all right.'

'You are a Pandit, right?'

'Yes.'

'I could make out from your nose that you are a Kashmiri.'

I smiled and, embarrassed, touched my nose.

'We are Hanjis. There used to be tribes in Kashmir earlier. We are one of those tribes. We made the water our home. We and the Pandits have been here for a long time.'

In everything there is a glimpse of the past here. Rooh used to say, 'No matter how hard you try to run away from this, it is a fact that you are a part of the past of this place.'

I want to see Kashmir in front of me now, but my eyes keep searching for the past. My eyes are least interested in the present. They want to live in the past.

'I was born in Khwaja Bagh.'

'So, you will go there?'

'I don't know.'

'Do you have anything left there?'

I didn't respond to that. What remains after leaving from anywhere? And if at all something remains, why should it be hoped that one would return some day? It's also been twenty-seven years since 'I will return one day'. I couldn't see anything the last time I'd visited for a few hours. It was so overwhelming for me that it felt as if I was again in a dream and someone would wake me up.

'Actually, I don't want to go there.'

'Why?'

'What will I do? How much will I be able to gather?'

'If you are able to gather anything, where will you take it?'

What were we talking about? When I looked towards him, he stood facing the chinars on the other side of the lake.

'The shikara owner, who had come to sell flowers during the day, also sells their seeds to the tourists. He also has the seeds of chinar, and the fun bit is that people buy them and take them along. They try to grow these trees with their distinct methods in Mumbai and Delhi. But if you see a chinar in Mumbai or Delhi, will you feel good or bad about it? Tell me.'

I remained quiet. I was suddenly reminded of my father.

'Most probably it won't grow. If at all it does, it will die quickly.' Basheer finished our conversation with this. Then he took his small boat and began to row towards his home on the other end of the Nigeen Lake. As soon as he left, I carried my drink and moved to the deck of the bigger houseboat. Gul's houseboat was at the extreme end of Nigeen Lake. There was no other movement visible around me, no sounds other than the sound of the azan wafting in from a distance. Every now and then, when the wind blew stronger, the sound of the water striking the houseboat was audible. I lay on my back on the deck and began to gaze at the stars. Six years ago, too, I had lain here in a similar fashion.

Rooh always carried a book with her. I had never seen her without a book. I read as much fiction as she used to read non-fiction; maybe that was why we got along very well. When she would tell me about a non-fiction book, I would tell her a fictional tale about the same subject. But when she spoke about Kashmir, I would go silent. Neither of us had slept that night in New York. We were up with our wine bottle till we saw the sunrise from the bank of the Hudson River. That night, I had promised Rooh that if she came to India I would take her to Kashmir. She had said that she could come along right away, but first she wanted to read more about Kashmir, 'When I am ready I shall let you know,' she had said.

Two years after New York, we had come here and stayed in this house boat. She had actually come fully prepared.

She had said, 'May I tell you something funny about Kashmir?'

'Yes, please.'

'They have always sought support from others for the barbarities committed against the Kashmiris. They had called the Afghans to fight the Mughals, so that there would be peace in the valley. Then they called the Sikhs to fight the Afghans, but the problems of native Kashmiris never ended.'

She had laughed a lot at this.

'Where do you find all this?'

'One has to read. You want to hear more?'

'Yes.'

'I hope you are not too sensitive to get annoyed later?'

'If I were sensitive, I would have been annoyed by now thinking how come I don't know all this about Kashmir.'

'Okay, listen. The Kashmiris are actually very simple. But along with being simple, they tell a lot of lies. It is difficult to catch their lies. Walter Roper Lawrence wrote in *The Valley of Kashmir*, "Kashmiris did not strictly adhere to the truth, and attributed their misery to lying, envy or malice." About a century later, V.S. Naipaul mentioned Aziz and Mr Bhatt in his book, and said something similar. Their simplicity is extremely cute. Like during the militancy, when all the jails were full, even if there was a little suspicion on anyone, they were thrown into jail for interrogation. But nobody would say anything. Then the army allowed them to meet their families in a separate tent once a week. There they had put microphones, and thus the army would get detailed descriptions of all the militant operations. Then an army officer installed a dummy computer for interrogation, which had a printer attached to it that printed a graph like that of the heartbeat. A man wearing white clothes would sit at that machine. The moment the officer felt that a person was lying in the interrogation, he would indicate the same to this man on the machine. The printer would start running and the officer would say, "The computer is saying that you are lying." After a while they would blurt out all the truth. This "Truth Machine" had become so famous that once a terrorist was caught with his lover, and the officer told him that if he didn't tell them the truth, he would switch on this "Truth Machine" and call his wife. The ferocious terrorist was so scared that he started working for the army. And then once . . .'

'Enough, enough.'

I was about to laugh, but I didn't want to hear any more.

Rooh said jokingly, 'I can see someone here is really sensitive!'

'I am experiencing this fragrance of Kashmir after years. I am scared I might lose it by reading more.'

'All right, so I will tell you the good things.'

'How many books have you read?'

'I told you I shall come fully prepared.'

Then she began listing the good things, and I didn't realize when the night got over.

Today, the night hasn't even begun, and it seems as if a long time has passed. Just then Shabeer called.

'Salaam, bhai! I have come to Srinagar.'

'Oh! What are you doing here?'

'I have come to attend a wedding. You have to come. Wazwan will be served tomorrow.'

'Sure. Where?'

'I shall send you the address.'

Suddenly, I felt charged up. I left the deck, rushed to my room and began to work on my novel on my laptop. This was strange; every time I felt a sense of belonging to Kashmir, I was able to get back to working on my novel. This novel is about a sixth-standard child who has nothing to do with Kashmir. A sense of belonging leads makes you feel at ease, and in that ease your imagination can leap over mountains. This works in the opposite way as well; whenever the novel opens itself easily, I open another folder and start writing about Kashmir. When I come to one from the other, the first one sits beside me like a good friend listening about this new life of the other one. In our living, our life, we are simultaneously living multiple lives. Our stay in every city has a distinct tale. In each new relationship, an old relationship sits beside an old friend who keeps whispering. I often think about what our life is. What do I want to actually write? Is there something real about life? Real writing? Or maybe the real just comes and goes in our imagination?

When militancy had begun to spread its wings in Kashmir, we had moved to Hoshangabad, but my father was still there because of his job. He thought that if he stayed back, he would be able to save some money. Nobody had imagined that the situation in Kashmir would worsen as much as it did. The JKLF had conveyed to all Pandits, via newspapers, pamphlets, and announcements from masjids, that Kashmir was going to be a Muslim nation and that they should leave. Kashmir had witnessed so many upheavals, but nobody had imagined that this was ever possible. Every person waited for this bad phase to pass, trusting their neighbours. Then people began to die, and that seemed like the end of all possibilities.

Father was called to the Rainawari home because there were only women in the house, and men were needed in this situation. Father took over the responsibility of getting everyone out from there, and, one by one, everyone began to pack up and leave. When my father was the last one left, he again thought about the money. He thought that if he could save some more money, it would be useful for the family. He had applied for an advance salary of a few months in his office, and he wanted to wait for it. Just then, militants came to burn down the government handicraft office close to our house in Rainawari. That fire could have also reached all the homes around it. Fearlessly, Father just stepped out and began to shout at the militants. Some of our Muslim neighbours understood the gravity of the situation and pulled him inside, though by then the militants had taken notice of my father. The militants now knew that a Kashmiri Pandit was living in this house; maybe this scared the neighbours too. Father would now sleep at night with complete blackout. The neighbours would send him meals. At night, he would put a candle on the first step of the house, so that light would not show outside. He now gave up the hope of getting his advance salary and tried to leave, but by then circumstances had worsened further and his getting out also seemed difficult.

Mother was not getting any letters from Father. Whatever news about Kashmir reached Hoshangabad, it was dreadful. My mother had never stepped out of the house, but she decided she would go to Bhopal and request the governor for assistance. When she reached the governor's office, she was told that the governor doesn't meet anyone without an appointment. Mother sat outside the office with both her children, and when she couldn't think of anything else, she began to cry. She couldn't understand where she could go now; everyone was eerily silent about Kashmir. Someone informed the governor that a Kashmiri woman was sitting outside crying, with her two kids. He immediately called her inside. We came to know that the governor's name was Qureshi, a Kashmiri Muslim. Before he listened to mother's plea, he offered her water, ordered some tea for her and then asked her what the issue was. Mother gave him all the details. Qureshi Sahab contacted the BSF right there in front of Mother and initiated the procedure to extract our father from there.

A few days later, a policeman came home and gave her Rs 10,000 that had been sent by Qureshi Sahab. Because of Qureshi Sahab, our father reached Hoshangabad safely after some days.

When Mother retold this story, she insisted that Kashmiri Hindus and Kashmiri Muslims were like members of the same family—both looked the same, both spoke the same language, their food was the same, and they even celebrated their festivals together. We would all gather at the meat shop—us, having come out of our temples; and they, having stepped out of their masjids. Mother was not a Kashmiri. She had made Kashmir her own, and her list of such examples of peaceful coexistence was long.

I came to know through Rooh that there were hundreds of books on Kashmiri history. The history of Kashmir, from ancient to recent times, has been well documented. What I am writing is just connected to those images that I have lost. Just like Rooh had said, that I was a part of Kashmir's past, so I am writing just my minuscule part from that expansive past. In this quest I want to reach where I was born. I just want to touch that sky, that colony, that blue door and those white walls once.

As I came out of the houseboat holding my coffee, I saw Basheer coming towards me in his shikara. He waved a small packet at me, and I understood that he was getting me some warm and fresh lavas. The insurmountable exertion of constantly turning from side to side during the night began to shake off as I saw him smile. He anchored his shikara and began to hurriedly head towards the kitchen.

'You wake up so early. What are you having? Who made this? Wait, let me make some noon chai for you.'

He was least interested in my response and entered the kitchen muttering constantly.

It had rained at night. The mountain peaks that surround Srinagar on one side looked dusty. The water of the Nigeen Lake was so calm that the conversations rising from within had changed into whispers.

When I was growing up, I had enrolled myself for blood donation. Every few days I would get a call from there telling me that it was my turn to donate blood at so and so place. Once, I was sitting among Kashmiri relatives after donating blood. The cotton swab was still stuck to my arm. Some of the Kashmiri relatives had seen that and total pandemonium ensued!

'Don't you know how pure Kashmiri blood is?'

'Are you aware how many years it takes to form one drop of Kashmiri blood?'

'This thankless fellow just donated a full bottle!'

'Blood like ours is not found anywhere else.'

'He wouldn't know because he is only a half-blood Kashmiri.'

'Poor fellow has been fooled.'

'He is stupid.'

I think I was in the tenth standard and used to listening to such sentences. My mother would always instruct me to stay quiet at such gatherings. We were the outsiders here as well. They all began sentences addressing us with the phrase 'poor things'. I had come to realize at a very young age that I didn't belong anywhere. In Hoshangabad, both of us brothers looked different. Even though we were bathing less frequently, we were teased, and at Kashmiri gatherings we were overlooked. When I mentioned this to Rooh she told me, 'You know, the idea of forming Pakistan began with something similar. There, too, a major role was played by a Kashmiri Pandit.'

How did Rooh have all the answers? I wonder, even today. She told me about Muhammad Iqbal, who later became famous as the poet Allama Iqbal. He belonged to a Kashmiri Pandit family— Sapru Sialkotwale—and much later he converted to Islam. Allama Iqbal's paternal grandfather was Kanhaiya Lal, who was married to Poshi. She was named Indrani after her marriage. They had three children: Ratan Lal, Nand Lal and Bihari Lal. Ratan Lal was Allama Iqbal's father. He fell in love with a Muslim girl of his locality, and he married her. His family gave up on him. Ratan Lal converted to Islam and became Noor Mohammed. When Iqbal was growing up, he tried to work on a truce in his family. He met his grandfather and Indrani, and told them that he was also from the bloodline of Saprus (Kashmiri Pandits). But because his mother was a Muslim, neither her family nor his father's family accepted him. Iqbal wasn't too happy with his father, and he had told his grandmother Indrani this. She cried a lot, but she could not make Iqbal a part of her family. Iqbal left seething in anger. Long after Iqbal left, Indrani thought he must be sitting outside the door. If the Sapru family had accepted Iqbal, maybe the history of India and Pakistan would have been different. Khushwant Singh has written somewhere: 'Those who are first-generation converts are usually fundamentalists.' Iqbal had also become a Muslim fundamentalist.

Iqbal had become a major ideologue demanding Pakistan. Iqbal had recited this poem of his in a Kashmiri conference:

> *Oppression and ignorance hold us under their claws*
> *Our wings have been clipped as if by scissors*

God, break the hands of the persecutor
Who rides roughshod on Kashmiris' soul!

Iqbal died on 21 April 1938, nine years before the formation
of Pakistan.

On a morning like this one, Rooh had told me all this about
Iqbal. I used to wonder how she remembered it all.

'You also turned out to be a poet, but that anger kept you
distanced from your Kashmiriyat.'

I wanted to argue about this with Rooh. But what could I say?
All her claims were correct.

'I feel this is a far more complicated matter and not as simple as
you are making it out to be.'

'I am even more distanced than you. I know only what I have
read, whereas you have lived it, so you might know better.'

She knew better. I was just a mad man overwhelmed by my
feelings. If it had been Rooh instead of me who had lived what I
had, she would have written the most beautiful book on Kashmir
ever. What I am writing is more like the mutterings of an old man
that are largely for himself.

'Here is your noon chai and lavas.'

Basheer quickly removed the cup of my black coffee before me.
The noon chai was very good; the lavas had turned cold but still
tasted good with the noon chai.

'What's the plan for today?'

'I have been invited to a wedding.'

'Oh! You shall have Wazwan today.'

'Yes.'

'Then don't eat anything else after these lavas. Be on an
empty stomach.'

'That's what I intend to do.'

I kept circling around my novel the entire day. I would write a
few words intermittently, and a few sentences would be kind enough
to come and fill in the blank spaces. When I was about to leave,
I thought I look so unlike a writer. But what does a writer look like?

Basheer had said that my nose is Kashmiri. I am Kashmiri in parts. But what about the other parts of me?

Sometimes, I would see Basheer around, and at other times I would feel as if I was the owner of these three houseboats. There were apples on the trees in the backyard. I was so hungry that I had already eaten two apples. Around one o'clock I went across the lake. Mushtaq was waiting for me there.

'You must have been feeling very bad without me,' Mushtaq said as soon as we met.

'Yes, I was struggling without you.'

'If you really insist, then I shall stay back with you this time.'

We both laughed a lot at this. Mushtaq had come all dressed up.

'You know I am a Pandit from my mother's side and a Muslim from my father's side.'

'The opposite of Allama Iqbal.'

How difficult is it to determine who's who among us humans? Which human community is the best, and for how long has this conflict continued? How much blood has been shed to resolve this? If we take religion away, can the weak and the strong not survive together? Where is the end of this war about proving masculinity and being the best? When all this gets tainted by religion, it gets even worse.

We were about to reach Chaanpura. It was around three o'clock, and I was terribly hungry. Mushtaq was busy talking to his relatives on the phone. He had to take many people back to Anantnag with him. When we reached the house where the wedding was taking place, the women were having Wazwan. After greetings, Shabeer took me to a room inside. All around there were well-dressed men, women and kids. The fragrance from outside was such that Shabeer and I were already waiting impatiently, literally clutching our stomachs. Then he took me to the rear side, where the Wazwan was being made. It was being made in huge vessels on wooden fire, as per Kashmiri tradition. Looking at the boiling yakhni, rogan josh, keema, paneer, saag, I thought about how diverse and rich our country is in its food and colours. Unparalleled diversity. And it is this diversity that makes this country different from others. I feel proud of my country in such moments. Any Kashmiri's eyes will moisten when he gets traditional food.

After a long wait, Shabeer whispered to me that the tent was ready for the men to have their meal. The bride had gone, and now the groom was seated on the stage with his friends. People began to sit in circles of four. As soon as they sat, a huge, round, covered plate was placed before them. The moment the lid of the plate between the four of us was removed, a strong fragrance touched my being. My mouth watered instantly. The plate already had a lot of chicken, meat, rice and kebabs, and they had given everyone a bag to carry any leftovers home. I looked around and saw that people were keeping most of the food in their bags, but I was eating the Wazwan for the first time, so I wanted to taste everything. A child was sitting next to me. The moment I extended my hand towards the chicken he said, 'Why are you killing your appetite? Taste the meat first.' He was right. He said again, 'Wait for yakhni or your stomach will get full already.' I could not wait for anything. I began to change my way of sitting midway through the Wazwan. My hunger had been satiated but not my desire. I was just gulping down food. Shabeer told me that the original Wazwan had only seven kinds of food. But as people got richer, they began to add more things to show off. At some weddings, thirty-five kinds of food were served. This is sheer madness.

By the time the Wazwan was over I was in no condition to even move. Just then I saw Shabeer's father. This time I could not stop myself and I hugged him.

'How are you? Did you eat well?'

'Ji, I ate too much too well.'

'Come home.'

'No, I shall go back right now. I have to write a lot.'

'When will you come?'

'Before I leave.'

'All right, I shall wait for you.'

I knew I would not meet him again. I knew that it was probably my last meeting with him. Yet, holding on to hope and waiting has become my habit, and I can't get rid of it.

Everyone had eaten so much that nobody was in a condition to talk to anyone. Shabeer came to see me off outside, up to the autorickshaw. I hugged Shabeer and said thank you to him, and then I set off for my place.

The auto driver was a young boy. His clothing indicated that he did something else for a living too. He stopped the auto at a shop; a friend of his came running and sat with him in the driver's seat. Now there were three of us in the auto heading towards Nigeen Lake. They were both chatting with each other and would often include me in their conversation. I told them that I was also from Kashmir and a Pandit, and, as it usually happens, the conversation then became heavy.

'After the repeal of Section 370, we were imprisoned for about six months in our own homes,' the boy who had come later said.

'We were not consulted at all about it. A decision was just forced on us. Everyone here felt cheated,' the auto driver added.

I had nothing to say to them. They were the ones living here; I could only listen to them.

Trying to divert the topic, I said, 'Your work must have been affected a lot?'

'Yes, 370 first and then Covid. Everyone here has been down in the dumps.'

'It is good that everything is gradually normalizing,' I added with a smile.

'They shall not spare anyone who buys lands here, and those who sell their land, their entire family shall be in danger,' the auto driver's friend said.

'Who are they?'

They both turned around at my question, as if I had asked something extremely stupid.

'There was a famous dhaba at Dal Lake. He sold it to outsiders, and they executed his son. He was our friend, what can be done now?' said the auto driver.

We were passing through a lot of army camps. Just then I realized that we were in Rainawari, and my gaze shifted to the sky. The same kites were there; in my childhood, I had left the place watching them.

'Please don't be offended by what we say. You are our Kashmiri brother and must be aware of what we go through here.'

'I cannot understand, but I can feel it.'

'That's enough,' said the auto driver.

We had reached ghat number one of Nigeen Lake. The auto driver asked, 'What do you do?'

'I am a writer.'

'You don't look like one.'

'That's what I have to work on.'

They both began to laugh at this. They must have been half my age. Both of them seemed to have several dreams in their eyes, the faith to achieve something in the improbabilities of a future. Hope makes all humans beautiful. I shook hands with both of them and sent them off with some extra money.

'Maybe you had to leave in order to really miss a place; maybe you had to travel to figure out how beloved your starting point was.'

—Jodi Picoult

Now I understand why my father never spoke about Kashmir. Each person here has their own Kashmir with which their past is intricately entwined. Each event can have as many versions as the number of people narrating it. One doesn't even get to know when the personal becomes public and when the public robs you off the personal. 'Future' is the least-mentioned word, because the future is so dicey. So much so that till the present is lived with full freedom, any assertion about the future will sound like a lie.

Lal Ded has written:

Some, who have closed their eyes, are wide awake.
Some, who look out at the world, are fast asleep.
Some who bathe in sacred pools remain dirty.
Some are at home in the world but keep their hands clean.

After I returned, I kept roaming on the deck for a long time. I always remain restless when I'm trying to write, or, one can say, when one can't comprehend what is being written. Whatever I am writing right now about Kashmir is sounding like my life, which is not heading anywhere, particularly right now. I should be sitting in front of my laptop right now, whereas I am walking around in circles.

At night, Basheer got the keys to the room where Rooh and I had stayed.

'You seem quite upset today. Go and sleep there. You will feel better.'

This time I did not refuse. I took the keys and began to walk towards the room.

Basheer called out behind me, 'I shall bring your drink and cigarette there.'

What right do you have over your birthplace? What right does that place have over you? Can anyone ever ask for their rights? My estrangement with Kashmir continued, which was justified because I neither knew the language nor was I familiar with its history, and I hadn't turned back to it for thirty long years. I was occupied in my struggles to get accepted by Hoshangabad. And just when I began making close friends, I left that city too. When I arrived in Mumbai I was a small-town boy who would fake laughter at English jokes and later keep asking for the meaning of each word. I have never even considered belonging fully to one place important. I have written this in my previous travelogue as well, that language is not essential for establishing a connection. But now that I have set out to capture the images of my past, everything is sounding and appearing strange. I was looking at my own past through new lenses. Maybe this was a result of the fresh turmoil in Kashmir. There is this instability of some kind which is forcing me to look at my own life from a different angle.

Basheer came and gave me a drink and some cigarettes. That room of the houseboat was just the same, except there was no bukhari here. The room used to have the soft warmth of belongingness due to the bukhari—my soul and I were lying cold here. Its emptiness seemed strange right now. I had opened the windows of the room. I sat on the window ledge with my drink and cigarettes, with my feet down towards the lake. There is a constant struggle between new experiences and the urge to experience the same things and the place as it was once. With every sip of the drink I was alone, and with every puff of my cigarette, I felt that Rooh was somewhere close by. Rooh would delve deep into a subject and talk about it. I would emphasize more on the emotional aspect. Either my imagination would totally collapse around her or it found a new direction altogether. She said once, 'You must write something about Kashmir someday.'

'I do write about it, Kashmir. It lies scattered in whatever I write.'

'No, not scattered but gathered.'

'What does that mean?'

'It means whatever you say about Kashmir to me, the same stuff as it is.'

'But that would be like a private, emotional conversation. There must be something else written about Kashmir that makes people understand every aspect of it.'

'There has been a lot written about Kashmir and still being written. This private, emotional conversation is something I would like to read about.'

'I shall try.'

'If you don't, then Kashmir will keep bothering you again and again in whatever you write.'

'And you will also keep bothering me.'

'No, I will be gone after leaving Kashmir.'

She had said this smiling. But I had no doubt that Rooh had not hidden anything. We only had time till Kashmir, and maybe that was why we were both so open and loyal to each other. Rooh had told me this when I had asked her if we could remain in touch even after leaving Kashmir. Rooh loved to live the intensity of a relationship; she also loved history a lot, and with me she was living both. She had said, 'There is no reason for us to be together after this Kashmir trip is over.' This was true to an extent.

'I will try to write,' I had told her.

'But you can't write about Kashmir living in Mumbai.'

'Then where do I write about it?'

'You will have to come here.'

'I don't think that is important,' I had said, almost interrupting her.

'Nothing is important. If we were having this conversation in New York, it would be so fake in a way. Here in Kashmir, its fragrance, its taste is maintained in our interactions almost effortlessly.'

'Can I write now?'

'You can try, but I feel you would not be able to write now.'

'Why?'

'I don't know.'

I tried to write but I wasn't able to. Then I tried to write about Rooh but was unsuccessful in that as well. Maybe one needs to distance oneself even from one's soul to write about it. I took a deep breath. I was feeling calmer in this room. Ever since I had entered Kashmir, there had been a strange discomfort. Tonight was perhaps the first night when I was fully comfortable. I must go to Khwaja Bagh. Why was I loitering in Srinagar? But maybe I wasn't in a condition to directly go to Khwaja Bagh. I decided that I would go to Gulmarg. Khwaja Bagh was about two hours away from there.

I must have been in the tenth or eleventh standard when I had organized a fashion show in Hoshangabad. Till then I had never even stepped out of Hoshangabad. I had heard the words 'fashion show' on TV. I understood it as showcasing clothes. Back then, I had been itching to do something new. Around that time, many boutiques had opened in our small towns. I thought that if I asked a few local boutiques to give their clothes for this fashion show, it would be something new for our small town. 'Shallow vessels make the most noise' seemed to fit me fully. A hall was booked for the event, and a few local celebrities were invited to judge the fashion show. All the boutique owners were excited, and ten girls from Hoshangabad also agreed to catwalk wearing different salwar-kameez sets.

Both the NSUI and ABVP were strong in Hoshangabad at that time. One day, a boy, who was an acquaintance, came home. I assumed he had come to have tea with me, so we sat and began to chat. He casually said, 'Don't organize this fashion show. It isn't right.' I assumed he was kidding, in a friendly way. I explained that it would be good for the boutiques of our city. But he suddenly became aggressive and began to throw words like 'culture' and 'tradition'. The conversation concluded with his threatening me that they won't let this event happen. Later I got to know that he was a member of a students' group, and this was a golden opportunity for him to rise in the ranks of his organization. Next day onwards, their protest was plastered on the walls of the city; there were announcements from a tonga that these Kashmiris were spoiling our culture. How my Kashmiri identity was relevant to this was beyond me! Our booking at the hall was cancelled, and whichever venue we tried to booked, it was cancelled the very next day. I thought maybe people were not getting what I was trying to do, so I started going to their homes to explain to them what it was all about. But I was shocked when I was told, 'You are the Kashmiris who were chased away from there, and now you will be thrown out from here too. Why don't you go back to your Kashmir? Why are you spoiling our city?'

I would keep looking at people in shock. I knew these people; their children were my friends. How could they say such things to me? But this was happening for real. Finally, we decided we would do the fashion show. Right at the crossing there was an under-construction shop. I didn't even know the owner. He said, 'Take my shop, and do your fashion show here.' All my friends joined me, even those whose parents had said hurtful things to me. We created a stage by joining the shop to the road and created space for the audience to sit. The event happened with great pomp and show. So much controversy had surrounded the show that people had poured in to see it. All the girls, who had been getting all kinds of threats, too, did not back out and participated in the show. They walked the stage with flair, wearing all those clothes.

The fashion show did happen, but the walls of the village had a message painted on them that stayed for long: 'Go Back Kashmiri.' Every now and then I would see that. One day, I asked my father, 'If we are chased away from here, can we go back to Kashmir? Or will we have to look for another place to live in?' My father did not respond. Now, here in Kashmir, I can comprehend his silence. By spending just some time in Kashmir, I have begun to understand how and when we become quiet. The silence resembled my father.

I got up very early in the morning and packed my things. I had decided that I should be closer to Khwaja Bagh, Baramulla. I was waiting for Basheer's shikara. As soon as I saw him approaching, I waved to him, and he waved back the packet of lavas at me. When he was tying his shikara I told him, 'Please get me a cab. I want to go to Gulmarg.'

'Have tea first, then we shall talk,' he said.

He tied the shikara and went straight to the kitchen. I was surprised. What was there to talk about in this? I went to my room and got my luggage out, so that Basheer understood that I was serious about this. Basheer was standing outside with the noon chai and lavas. I took them from him and sat on the stairs of the boat house. The morning sun was warming my face. The bread and tea were adding to the flavour of this morning.

'Why do you want to go to Gulmarg?'

'I will write there, and then go to Khwaja Bagh from there.'

Though there was no need to answer him, Basheer had this sense of entitlement in his tone, and I couldn't make my way around it.

'Then go straight to Khwaja Bagh.'

'No, I shall first write for a few days in Gulmarg and then go to Khwaja Bagh from there.'

'Gulmarg would be crowded. If you have to go to Khwaja Bagh after a few days, I can tell you where to go now.'

He said this and went inside. There was a diary in his hands. He looked up a number in the diary, dialled it and had a long conversation in Kashmiri. My tea was in my hand, and the piece of bread that I had broken was still stuck in my mouth. I knew that he was talking to someone about me. After a while he said goodbye and disconnected the call.

'He will be here in half an hour.'

'Who?'

'The driver.'

'What for?'

'He shall take you to Aaru.'

I instantly searched for Aaru on my phone.

'Oh! This is towards Pahalgam, in the opposite direction from Baramulla.'

'Yes.'

'But I have to go towards Baramulla.'

'You don't want to go to Baramulla. Go to Aaru for a few days, work there. It is a nice place.'

He went again to the kitchen. I kept looking at him in shock. Now, in half an hour, I was going to Aaru, Pahalgam, something I had no idea about before that moment.

'Where will I live there? At least tell me that,' I shouted.

'There are many hotels there. The driver shall take you,' Basheer shouted back.

Shortly afterwards, I could hear Basheer arguing with someone from the kitchen. I was standing outside with my things. When he came out his face was red.

'What happened?'

'The driver isn't coming. Finding a small car is a problem here. Come, I shall drop you.'

'What does "come" mean? You will leave your entire business to drop me to Aaru?'

'No, I shall drop you till Dal Gate. From there you can take a shared cab and go.'

'Shared cab?'

'Everyone here takes them.'

'But I can pay for a taxi.'

'Why spend unnecessarily?'

He picked up my things and began to walk out. I took my bags from him.

'You walk ahead. I shall pick these up.'

The weather had changed suddenly; it was drizzling. Basheer dropped me off at the Dal Gate. It was slightly crowded there.

He went straight to the driver of the shared cab and then came back to me. 'It will cost you one hundred and twenty rupees. They shall drop you up to Islamabad.'

'How will I go further to Pahalgam from Anantnag and then to Aaru?'

'Even if you took a cab, it would drop you up to Pahalgam only. From there you would have to hire a local vehicle.'

'All right.' I was angry at him but didn't want to show it. I gave my haversack to the taxi owner.

'Can I put this on the top? If the stuff gets wet and soiled, it isn't our responsibility.'

'Keep it. Let it all get soiled,' I said and began to walk towards the car.

Basheer called out, 'Will you go just like that?'

He was standing with his arms outstretched. I went and hugged him. When Basheer spoke with this kind of entitlement he sounded like a father. His hug also had the warmth of a father.

'Next time, come sooner,' he said as he left.

The cab left after about half an hour. There were three people in the front seat. I immediately called Mushtaq.

'Mushtaq, I need you. I shall be reaching Anantnag. Can you take me further to Aaru?'

'Definitely. I am overjoyed that you called. If you wish, I will also stay with you.'

'No, just drop me there. I have just left from here. So I will see you in about an hour.'

'Right.'

Then I called Shabeer and told him that I was coming to his restaurant for tea. He was happy about it too.

Suddenly, I began to like all this. I wanted to thank Basheer, but I thought I shall do that when I reach Aaru. Mushtaq was waiting for me at the bus station at Islamabad (Anantnag). His eyes were shining. We went to Shabeer's restaurant. He was waiting for us with bread and tea.

'How is your writing proceeding?' asked Shabeer as soon as we met.

'It has proceeded up to you.'

'That means it is headed in the right direction.'

'It seems so.'

Shabeer, Mushtaq and I laughed a lot while having tea. I read out some portions of what I had written; they seemed curious about it. But I noticed Mushtaq had become quiet, especially listening to the sections where I'd mentioned my childhood. As soon as we finished our tea, with the promise of seeing Shabeer again soon, Mushtaq and I set out for Aaru. For a long time Mushraq remained quiet; this wasn't normal. I also didn't say anything to him. He began to speak after a while. Now I don't know whether to narrate this tale further or not. Because after sharing his thoughts, Mushtaq stopped the car; his eyes were wet, and he was shaking. I told him that I might include his story in my book, but he didn't say anything. He seemed to be afraid of something, and I could understand that.

I said, 'All right, I will not write about it, but I do want to capture the images of your childhood—without naming anyone.'

He asked me to promise him that. I did, holding his hand—his hand was extremely cold. The fears of his childhood were still alive in him to such a great extent. I didn't know how I could write about them properly. A lot of time passed trying to decide what parts I could include and what parts to exclude. I am only narrating what I remember now, and what I feel is important and has to be told.

Mushtaq had said, 'After you all had left, the Kashmiris left behind suffered a lot. I was very young, and a lot of it is now mixed up in my head. Yet there are certain incidents that are difficult to detach from one's memory. I feel that it would be an achievement if anyone from my age group, who grew up in those times in the Valley, has good mental health now. I was in the fourth or fifth standard when I saw JKLF roaming in our village carrying guns. In a few years they became weaker, and everyone knows the reasons. Hizb-ul-Mujahideen had begun to spread their wings in Kashmir. They began to take their guns back from the JKLF, which was fighting for a free Kashmir, and began to claim that this was a crusade for Islam and they would take this up. Hizb-ul would come to our village and forcibly take everyone for Friday namaz to the masjid. Once they dragged me from my school. I wasn't even able to remove my shoes before entering the mosque. They wanted everyone to become their kind of Muslim. We had a small village. My father was a teacher; everyone knew everyone else, but times were such that anyone could be killed for simply taking any side. A new party emerged just then, Muslim Mujhaideen, which was determined to free Kashmiri people from the terror of Hizb-ul. They were getting support from RAW. Now, our village was caught in a strange triangle—JKLF, Hizb-ul and MM. My maternal village was under the control of Hizb-ul. Our village was dominated by MM. I have played with AK-47, machine guns and small guns in childhood. They allowed the children to clean their guns. We kids would compete among ourselves about who had how many empty bullet shells. I have fired guns instead of crackers for Eid.

Hizb-ul wanted to kill the people associated with MM, and MM wanted to destroy Hizb-ul. Once Hizb-ul distributed pamphlets in the village saying nobody should switch off their lights at night. MM distributed pamphlets saying nobody must have their lights on. My father got all the windows covered with bricks, leaving just a gap of a single brick for air, and that too was covered with a wire mesh. We would switch on the light at night, but since our home was closed on all sides, no light would go out. Common Kashmiris had to find ways to guard themselves from both the groups. Sounds of gunfire and grenade blasts at night were common. Once, I went to the village with my maternal grandmother and saw the house was on fire. I had a trunk there, in which we stored rice. It was upturned and burning. I haven't forgotten the sight of that fire till today. I had seen my friend burn. The grief of seeing a dear one die had become so normalized, as if we were talking about the death of a stranger. Then I saw Afghans in my village, seven feet tall, huge men and a few foreigners who could only speak English. I was too young; I couldn't find the courage to ask anyone who they were and why they were in our village. Once a militant threw a grenade on an army bunker; the grenade hit the mesh and exploded on the ground. I was returning from school at that time. The army opened machine-gun fire. I lay down where I was; I could feel the bullets whizzing past over me. It is in my blood to lie down on the ground as soon as I hear gunfire. Even now, if I hear bullets being fired somewhere, I would drop everything and lie down.'

Mushtaq stopped the car in the middle of the road but didn't get down. He was holding the steering wheel tightly. I asked him to park on the side, but he sat there like a statue. I got down from the car and walked a little distance away from him. He parked the car on the side eventually but didn't get out. I would have given him some more time, but it suddenly began to rain. I had to return to the car. We remained seated quietly in the car in the rain.

'I am sorry. I might have said too much,' Mushtaq whispered.

'No, it is all right. I can understand.'

When the car started moving again, I put my arm across Mushtaq's shoulder. Can we touch another person's fears? I was reading a book at that time—*Rumours of Spring* by Farah Bashir. It is an intimate tale of a girl growing up in the valley during the militancy. In Mushtaq's entire tale there was no mention of girls. There were a few incidents of rape. But why were the girls growing up along with the boys missing from these narratives? I had noticed this in interactions with almost everyone. I had spoken about this topic to a few people, and one person had suggested that it was because of the women that the militants weren't able to enter homes. Nothing much was written about those women.

'Listen, now you must narrate something wonderful to lighten the mood a bit,' Mushtaq suggested.

'I want to ask: What would have happened to the girls growing up along with you? When you can't get all this out of your thoughts, what they must have gone through is unimaginable for me.'

'I have seen girls rub the ashes from the stove on their faces, to blacken their fair skin. They were spared by none, neither the Hizbul nor MM.'

I couldn't speak after this, and neither could he. He put some songs on after a while. The songs that would have made me feel happy seemed hurtful at that moment. These old love songs sounded obscene now. When we reached Aaru, the cold along with the rain had increased. I began to feel good after entering the Aaru Valley. It was surrounded by tall mountains, on which the deodars were covered in dense fog.

I took a decent room at a decent hotel, dumped my stuff and went straight to the kitchen.

Both Mushtaq and I were very hungry. There was *batt** with Kashmiri *saag* and aloo matar—I had missed this simple yet delicious meal. After the meal I went to bid Mushtaq goodbye.

'I am not feeling too good. Can I have a kahwa with you?'

'Yes, sure.'

We both came to my room after ordering the kahwa. Till it was delivered, we both felt a strange heaviness inside us. Sipping the kahwa, Mushtaq said, 'You are almost my age, but you and I are so different.'

'I don't see much difference, Mushtaq. We are both on our own journeys.'

I was struggling for the right words. Mushtaq brushed them away with a sharp laugh. I became quiet.

'I often look at the children of the tourists who come to Kashmir. Especially foreign tourists—their food, their interactions with their parents and how they see this valley. Have you ever heard

---

* Rice.

their curious questions? I get this strange thought sometimes: Can we exchange all our children with those children?'

I had no answer to what Mushtaq was saying. He kept blabbering for a long time. The kahwa was over. I could hear Mushtaq's words in the room long after he had left.

My room was on the third floor. It was raining outside, and I could see the fog dancing among the trees on the mountains. I could not step out, but I was unable to settle in one spot. I found myself utterly alone. Deep silence, loneliness. My heart sank. I stopped pacing around. After some time, I found myself sitting on my haunches in my room. The laptop lay upturned on the bed. I didn't even want to touch it. I wanted to go out, talk to someone, make friends with someone, tell someone that I am utterly lonely. I wanted someone. I looked at my watch; time was crawling. But time runs faster in the hills! I got up again and began to walk around in my room. I wanted to be transported to some place where I wasn't this alone, if not in reality, at least in my head. Unwillingly, I picked up the laptop and began to peruse what I had written. Just then, when I looked out of the window, I felt as if I had seen a similar scene somewhere. Yes, I had stayed in some room in a small village in a French valley, Chamonix; my window overlooked Mont Blanc. In that room, too, I had a laptop in front of me. I would keep making coffee and writing my travelogue: *Bahut Dur Kitna Dur Hota Hai?* (How Far is Too Far?)

This thought made my heart sink even further. How much? How long? For whom? Why? Do I actually find pleasure in crawling alone like this? I had no answer to this. Everything had been okay till yesterday. This morning had also been fine. What was happening now? It felt as if my meticulously constructed castle of cards had collapsed. Nothing seemed to have any purpose. In the middle of 'I don't want anything' was a deep need for someone giving me some recourse, someone putting a hand on me and saying that I was not alone. I couldn't see what I had written. I closed the laptop and went to sleep, to find solace in bed. I wrapped myself in the quilt and began to look outside. There was no end to the rain. Everything was covered in darkness. Everything inside and outside now seemed to be wet. I picked up the phone wanting to call a friend, but whichever name I paused at, I felt too shallow to call them, and I put the phone away. I took a deep breath and thought I needed to step out. I tried to remove the quilt with all my strength, but my hands didn't obey me. So, even after a long while, I was still there, holding on to my phone, wrapped up in the quilt, looking outside.

I don't know how much time had passed before I could somehow gather up the pieces of myself and carry the burden of my loneliness downstairs to the kitchen. It was an energetic place—people were cooking, people were taking orders on their phones, and they still managed to place a cup of tea in front of me. Everybody dropped their Kashmiri and began to talk in Hindi, and, in no time, I had become a part of their discussions. Then I thought: Where has the loneliness gone now? Would it be waiting for me to step out, just outside the doorstep of the kitchen? I have been alone for so many days. Where had it been for so long?

'If you are lonely when you're alone, you are in bad company.'

—Jean-Paul Sartre

When I woke up in the morning everything was lighter. Outside, rain and clouds were still dancing together. On the vast darkness of the sky, there was a deep-blue spread. There was a sense of cold peace as far as the eye could see. Other than the rain and the clouds, everything was stagnant. I opened the laptop and began to read what I had written the previous day. The way I had described my loneliness, it now seemed like there was no need to write it into a travelogue about Kashmir. But travelling alone has its own highs and lows, and without experiencing this deep sense of complete loneliness, the journey remains incomplete. Hence it becomes important to describe this, as important as it is to describe all the other incredible experiences. Journeys are never simple. We must not say that journeys are simple, because we can't keep hiding our difficulties under the layers of these long journeys. It all tumbles out. All the aspects of a complex personality start showing up one by one. It is strange that this fluidity of the 'I' on these solo journeys, at times, forces one to navigate such tight emotional spots. The more we assume we have understood ourselves, the hazier we become for ourselves. And then, in some good moments, one feels the fog has lifted. It is all clearly visible, though one doesn't know how long this clarity would last. Just like this morning is cold and contains a deep peace.

'Just say it.'

Rooh and I were lying in bed.

'What should I say?' she asked.

'That funny thing that you were about to tell me but stopped.'

'Oh no, baba! You are very sensitive.'

'I'm not. Please.'

'In fact, I was also almost dying to tell you this.'

She sat up. Outside, ducks in the lake had come too close to the window of our boat. For a while, both of us kept looking at them. Then Rooh began to speak, 'In 1996 there were elections in Kashmir. The maulvi in the masjid at Shopian was delivering a public address, urging that nobody should vote. There were a lot of people in the masjid. An army officer arrived there with two of his men and asked the maulvi to not make these announcements from the PA system. The maulvi refused to obey. The officer asked his men to click pictures of all the people present in the masjid. For fear of being photographed, they stopped the announcements on the PA system immediately, and there was a near stampede inside. The rumour spread throughout Shopian. The next day, everyone turned out to vote, and all the people who were present in the masjid also went to show the officer the ink mark on their fingertip, proof that they had cast their vote.'

'We are actually cowards.'

Rooh looked at me softly, with affection.

'For the first time you have accepted your Kashmiri identity in front of me.'

'I will go and order coffee for you.'

Embarrassed, I was about to leave when Rooh caught hold of me.

'You have heard me. Now you also have to talk.'

'What, you have already heard it all.'

'You know how much I love to hear the stories of your childhood.'

I was back in bed. Now Rooh was lying down and I was sitting.

'When I used to crawl . . .'

'In Khwaja Bagh?'

'Yes. Once Ma was washing clothes in the bathroom. I crawled up to her and began to lick the laundry soap bar kept next to her. Ma didn't pay attention. After licking quite a bit of it, I crawled for some distance and then collapsed. After a long time, Ma realized that I had become unconscious. She quickly picked me up and rushed to the hospital.

When she reached the doctor at St Joseph hospital, he told her that the foam of the soap had reached my spinal cord. There was a slim chance of my surviving, and even if I did survive, I might have become paralyzed. My mother told the doctor it would be better for me to not survive rather than be paralyzed. The doctor hesitated a bit before saying, 'Let's wait and watch.' A lot of water was extracted out of my spinal cord. I was saved, but the doctor instructed that my head should be protected from any injury till I was at least ten. And I tell you, I have fallen head-first so many times in childhood: *Dham! Dham! Dham!*

I vividly remember that morning that I had spent with Rooh. The sunshine filtered through the small windows of the houseboat on our bed. In those lazy moments, whenever we touched each other, it seemed we were filling the blank spaces with our affection.

'Do you think your remaining single is also somehow related to Kashmir?' Rooh asked.

'Now you are overanalysing.'

'No, just think. Whenever you talk about Kashmir it is as if you are talking about an unrequited love. All your dreams are either of Kashmir or Hoshangabad. Whatever you feel close to you have lost. Maybe this acts as fear in all new relationships?'

'Maybe you are right.'

'Are you mad? I was just kidding, and you have become serious.'

That morning I was in love with Rooh. I was serious because I wanted that relationship to last. But Rooh was different; she knew what this relationship meant to her. Maybe the clarity she had, made me get far more intensely involved in this relationship than her. Whenever I would say sentences that seemed like love she would get scared. I couldn't see her scared.

In the Aaru Valley, I am right now the farthest from Khwaja Bagh. Khwaja Bagh is at the other end. The blue door and the white walls might still be there. Basheer was right in sending me here. There is still time for me to touch the threshold of my house.

It was sunny during the day. I left my room and went out into the grassy meadow. How familiar was this warmth of the sunrays on my body! I sat on the slightly wet grass. I could taste the fog, the moisture and the warmth of the sun in my breath. In Khwaja Bagh, where we had a front yard, Ma would do all her household chores outside with her best friend, Baby Aunty, if it was a sunny day. Baby Aunty would make me sit in her lap giving some excuse or the other. She had a lot of affection for me. Outsiders could mistake me for her son. She had always been a part of my dreams of Khwaja Bagh. Now, whenever I sat in the hills in the winter sun, I felt as if I was sitting in Baby Aunty's lap and Ma was sitting close by, knitting a sweater.

All the tourists were on the other side. This part of Aaru was quieter. The river flowed down there and the trees up on the mountain seemed to be engrossed in deep meditation. I was being reminded again and again of Mushtaq's words, 'After you all had left, the Kashmiris left behind suffered a lot.'

After 1988, whatever had transpired in this valley, and what the people who had left the valley had gone through—if all those stories are ever narrated, we would be ashamed of our humanity. Just like the Kashmiri Pandits living outside Kashmir explode when poked about this, similarly, the Kashmiri Muslims left behind explode when reminded of old incidents. But all this has not affected the love of Kashmiri Muslims for the Pandits or of the Pandits for the Kashmiri Muslims. The moment someone here comes to know that I am a Kashmiri Pandit, a bond of belongingness forms between us. The conversation that ensues is threaded by the belief, 'He knows everything.' The new generation of Pandits has only heard about what had happened; those who actually experienced it are either too old or dead. But the imprints of their life's experiences of those times are still visible on the faces of the Kashmiri Muslim kids who were growing up through it and the Pandit children who had not left.

'You all had left.' I understand the emotional gravity of this statement. As I sat by my father's side during his phone conversations with Gul Mohammed, the pain of being exiled from Kashmir was palpable to me. After so many years, when I was scratching the hardened Kashmiri soil inside me, with my nails, I was surprised to find that it was still moist. So where would my father have safely kept his Kashmir? I wondered. Maybe in his Godrej iron almirah, even peeping into which was prohibited for us. Before my father came back to us in Hoshangabad from Kashmir, this house of one room and a kitchen used to be always open. Its door was never shut. The windows remained open, and the neighbours could come and go at any time. When Father returned from Kashmir, he first put a thick wire mesh on all the windows; the door was reinforced and was always shut now. Before his return, we used to often put a bed outside and sleep—that stopped too. The four of us would sleep in a row in that room closed from all sides. There was a lot of difference between my father as he was in Kashmir and my father in Hoshangabad. Here, he would stay alert at all times, as if he always feared being cheated. He would keep looking for long at the people passing by. If someone passed by our house more than once, he would make a scary noise, so that they knew that they were being watched. We used to laugh a lot at this new father; we were just kids then and could never understand the deep meaning of this behaviour. He never mentioned what all he might have witnessed before leaving Kashmir. Who knows how much he had buried deep inside of him?

'You all had left.' I had picked the book *Rumors of Spring* because of this sentence. When Farah Bashir narrates about the pulling out of each hair by the root at night, it gives a deep insight into what the girls growing up in the valley in those times went through. Rooh had read much more. She knew as many stories about Kashmiri Muslims as she knew about the Pandits. She would often say, 'You must write about Kashmir.'

I would always evade this. I didn't even know much about the place.

'I don't have much to say.'

'As you begin to write, you would be surprised how much you have to share.'

'Those are just some fun incidents of childhood.'

'Then don't listen to me.'

'All right, I shall write someday.'

Sometimes, it so happens that some people come into your life for a short period of time, but they end up knowing you more than the people whom you have always lived with. I wish I could tell Rooh that I am in Kashmir right now and that I am writing. Maybe someday this book will be translated into English, and Rooh will get to know that I had come to Kashmir and that I wrote this here.

I might have been in class two at that time. A few of us were fooling around in the playground after the classes got over for the day. Just then, I saw a twenty-five-paisa coin on the ground. I quickly covered the coin with my foot. Everyone was having fun and going towards the school gate, but I didn't lift my foot. When the entire school was empty, I moved my foot, but the coin wasn't there. I cleaned the ground around it, looked around but couldn't find it anywhere. I sat there and began to cry, thinking I'd lost my twenty-five-paisa coin. My brother came back to look for me, but by then our bus had left. I told him, 'Let's walk home today. I know the way.' He trusted me. We were walking towards home but got lost. We didn't reach home, but after a long while we reached the bank of the Jhelum River. I was sure that we had lost our way. My brother asked me what I had been doing on the ground. I told him about the twenty-five-paisa incident. He also began to cry at this. We both stood on the riverbank, crying. One gentleman saw us. We described our address in broken sentences, and he dropped us home.

When Rooh watched the film *Hansa*, she noticed the twenty-five-paisa episode there. She had jumped with joy. She was right about Kashmir being present in everything I wrote or directed.

'I feel it is important to write personal narratives about Kashmir. There should be plenty of stories of Kashmir from all points of view. Our enemies are often those whom we don't know. It has been thirty years; it is only through these stories that we can embrace each other. It is in the stories that the skill of forgiving and being forgiven is hidden,' Rooh had said. We were strolling on the banks of Dal Lake at that time. She sounded so beautiful at sunset.

It was evening. The weather was clear, and there was no prediction of rain. I had come closer to the flowing water while strolling, but I spotted a group of tourists and began to climb back. I saw a small chai shop at the beginning of Aaru Bazaar. I ordered kahwa and girda and sat on the chair in the last row inside the shop. Just then, an old man, who had a spring in his step, entered the shop and ordered the same. That old man sat beside me, and as soon as our eyes met, he greeted me. Maybe he sensed my loneliness in the response I gave to his greeting. He now turned towards me. 'How long have you been here?' he asked.

'A few days.'

'And then?'

'What then?'

'Where will you go from here?'

'Baramulla.'

'Why?'

'Actually . . . I just want to leave.'

I didn't want to go through the tiresome process of narrating the entire story, hence I cut short my explanation.

'When will you leave?'

'Tomorrow morning.'

'Come with me. I am going to Gulmarg. I can drop you there and leave.'

'All right.'

I told him about my hotel and asked him to pick me up in the morning from there. After fixing all the details for the next day, as I left the place, I realized something unusual was happening on this journey. It was as if someone was watching over me, someone was helping me reach all the places. I didn't like this thought at all and returned to my room in a state of restlessness.

By morning, that restlessness had percolated into my body. I packed my stuff and came down to the kitchen to have tea and lavas.

I had not seen so much activity in the kitchen the morning before. I came to know one group had already left for trekking and another was about to leave. A man whom I had never seen before was standing in the centre of the kitchen and was loudly giving orders to others, and everybody was rushing about fulfilling his orders.

Two cups of tea arrived. One was handed over to me and the other to him. His name was Bilal.

'Why do you drink tea with so little milk?' He had asked this in Kashmiri, and I understood it.

'I am used to tea with less milk.'

Just then, somebody told him that I was a Kashmiri Pandit. Then they began to speak among themselves. I could only make out that they were talking about me.

'Where are you going?' Bilal asked, this time in Hindi.

'Right now, to Baramulla or Gulmarg. I don't know for sure as of now.'

'Oh! Why don't you accompany us on the Tarsar trek?'

'I would have come, but a man is going to come to pick me up.'

'Who?'

'I met him yesterday at the chai shop.'

'Okay, think about it. We are leaving now. This is your chance to see the real Kashmir.'

'But I have never been on a trek before, and I don't even have the clothes for it.'

'Tell me whether you want to do this or not. If you wish to come, everything can be arranged.'

I had finished my bread and chai. I don't know whether it was the enthusiasm in Bilal's offer or my own reluctance to go to Baramulla—I hesitated in taking a call. Then there was my discomfort with the thought that someone was trying to help me reach places. I came back to my room. My father's face appeared in front of me. Had he been around, I would have certainly asked him if my need to wander was actually rooted in Kashmir. I wanted to surrender with this restlessness in my body. But surrender before whom? How does one surrender? Can I go back and ask Rooh? Because only she knows it all. I suddenly began to question Rooh's existence. Is there something like *rooh* (soul) at all?

I gave Bilal some money. He brought me a cap, a light and a stick, and we set out for a four-day trek. There was a couple with me. Three of us began to climb up together. I didn't know their names until later. I had begun to huff and puff at the initial incline; my long-standing smoking habit was showing its results. Also, I didn't know how to trek. Before this, I had only attempted single-day hikes. In just half an hour we reached a thick forest of deodars. As I was walking, I thought about an old poem of mine, 'What shall we do with so much beauty?'

Bilal had gone further ahead on a horse. Three of us were behind him, taking baby steps along the way. Green meadows and sunlight filtering through the tall deodars would force us to stop again and again.

The boy said his name was Uday. I hesitantly told my name. The girl said her name was Iti. I began to laugh loudly. Iti and Uday—how was this possible? We three sat for a long time under a deodar and kept chatting. These two were surely not the Iti and Uday of my story. The Iti and Uday of my story wished to be just like them. These two were travellers in the true sense of the word. They had left their IT jobs and since then had been travelling constantly for the past year and a half; and next month they would move to Paris. Both spoke with each other intermittently in broken French. Uday told me that they had been quite scared as to who would be accompanying them for these four days. I could understand their anxiety; it is difficult to choose a co-traveller. I had taken up this journey with them without their permission.

After walking for almost two and a half to three hours, we reached our first halt: Green Lidderwat. We were at an altitude of 2970 metres, and the beautiful Lidder was flowing below, surrounded by tall mountains. We covered about ten kilometres. We had started late because of me, but still, we were almost on schedule. Bilal had set up the tent and started cooking. I had put away my things and was wandering. I had strayed from my journey, but I looked forward to this kind of straying. On the other bank of the river, one could see tree stumps and the beautiful homes of the settlement of Gujjars. I crossed the river using a bridge made of a single tree stump and began to head towards those homes. I entered a home, as a child had invited me in.

The child's mother was cooking on a *chulha*. All the kids sat surrounding her, and I sat on a raised mud platform with their father, Basheer. This was probably the space where they had their meals. They welcomed me as if they had been waiting for me. Basheer had just come back from Aaru. He distributed chocolates to all the kids. Soon there was noon chai and roti in front of me. The entire house smelt of smoke from the wood in the stove. These people lived here for six months and then shifted with all their things to Pahalgam in summers. The kids would study there for six months. One of Basheer's daughters was sitting next to me. She looked dirty, and her hair had not been combed, but she was extremely pretty. She had a deep tan due to playing in the sun. I began to think: What if she goes to the city when she's older? How would she stand among the girls studying in the big schools? These were my shallow urban thoughts, which stuck to me like the odour of sweat.

Next morning at seven, we started for Tarsar. Uday told me that we had to walk a lot that day. Bilal had handed all three of us food in tiffin boxes, and we had started climbing the high mountains. We found many homes, like Basheer's, on the way. There were several sheep, shepherds, horse owners, Bakarwals and Chopans on the way. By the time we reached Hamvas, Iti and I were in a bad shape. Uday had done many treks; he wasn't interested in resting. We had food at Sikwas and ran into people returning from Tarsar. I asked how far it was, and they said it was still a good distance away. They pointed towards a mountain and indicated that the Tarsar Lake was behind it. I felt intimidated looking at that mountain and thought it was impossible to get to Tarsar. Uday told me not to pay attention to the mountain and, instead, focus on my steps; he said we would be there soon. It was even tougher to move after having a meal. Uday was far ahead, and Iti and I were lagging behind.

It was getting overcast. Uday came running to us and said if the weather worsened, it would become even tougher to move; hence we had to move a bit faster. Iti and I looked at each other. We sat stuck to our spots. Uday took out some chocolate from his bag and offered it to us. As per his plan, I was now leading, and both of them were following me. I noticed he was discussing their plan to live in France with Iti. How would they make a home there, where would they live in Paris, what would they need to carry from here and what was more crucial to be learnt in the French class? Iti was completely engrossed in that conversation and distracted from the climb. I thought, Would I ever write the story of this Uday and this Iti?

Rooh couldn't read Hindi. She could understand very little, but she was constantly working at it. Every Hindi sentence that she spoke made me very happy.

She had said, 'I would never be able to know what you write. This makes me extremely sad.'

'But my book might have an English edition too.'

'But I want to read what you write in Hindi.'

I used to translate and narrate what I had written in Hindi into my bad English, but after a while it began to sound so strange that I had to stop.

'Okay, tell me. Is there no difference between running away and being chased away?' Rooh asked me, suddenly getting serious. We were in Gulmarg at that time. I was writing while sitting on the balcony of a cheap room, and she was in bed with her book and coffee.

'Yes, there is a huge difference.'

'Yesterday, at the dinner table, when you were talking to the waiters, and they were saying this again and again, that you had run away.'

'They are from Tangmarg. Maybe that's what they know.'

'But why didn't you say something?'

'What could I have said? My father was thrown out. But whenever I speak on behalf of my father, it feels like I am lying. These battles for territory, who was right and who was wrong . . . I have always found these discussions really crass. Do you remember I had told you about my play *Park*? The reason for writing it was this anger about how everyone is fighting for space and is so aggressive that he can kill the other. This, even when everyone has a bench in the park. There is space for everyone in this world.'

Rooh put her coffee down. She was disoriented by what I had said. She put the book on the table and came out to the balcony.

'In saying that you ran away, the entire blame is on you, and in being chased away it might be they who feel the burden of guilt on their shoulders. Everyone wants to get rid of this burden. Nobody wants to carry the burden of the past except the Germans. All of us have very cleverly used history for ourselves, and we are still doing it. As I am often told, my father was too simple, and his relatives looted him. But I haven't found a single relative till today who told me that the cheating relative was my father, who had looted everyone else.'

I had laughed a lot at this. Rooh could find humour even in the serious stuff.

Then, getting serious, she asked, 'Do you know what *raaliv, tasliv* and *ghaliv* mean?'

'Yes, raaliv means convert, tasliv means leave and ghaliv means die.'

'And do you know when were these used for the first time ever?'

'No.'

'Alexander, who was from the Shah Mir dynasty, 1389 to 1413 AD, had used it first against the Pandits. Many Hindus converted out of fear; many others left the Valley and several others were killed. At that time, somehow only eleven Hindu families survived in the Valley. No one must have imagined that after five centuries history would repeat itself.'

Every time she talked, I felt as if Rooh was more Kashmiri than me.

'But I know why you have come to Gulmarg?'

'Why?'

'I mean, you hate these touristy places, and yet here we are! Can you tell me why?'

'I thought you would like seeing the snow.'

She began to laugh. This laughter was to demolish my lie. I became quiet. I was very close to Baramulla. Khwaja Bagh was just two hours away from here.

'I can come with you to Khwaja Bagh, if you don't have a problem with it.'

'Let's see.'

I said that and began pretending to write again. Rooh kept sitting in front of me for a long time. How could I have lied to my Rooh and thought that I would not be caught?

At last, almost crawling, we reached Tarsar. Bilal had put up the tents, and he was making chai. I nearly fell in front of the tent. We had walked for seven hours, during which we had covered about fifteen kilometres and climbed one kilometre. I barely remember walking in a straight path. We were constantly climbing up, and were now at an altitude of 3950 metres. My legs had been drained of their strength, but I still wanted to see the Tarsar Lake. After tea, I walked towards it. Nature has such surprises in its treasure that even while looking at them one finds them unbelievable. It is so difficult to believe that such a huge blue lake exists, at such an altitude. I had to close my eyes for a while. Then I touched its cold water to make sure that what I was looking at was actually there. I sat at the edge of the lake on a rock. My eyes were wet. I took some pictures just for the sake of it. But not a single picture could do justice to the view in front of me. I put my mobile back in my pocket and returned to my tent.

I woke up at about three at night. I needed to pee. Just then I sensed the slightest movement outside my tent. It seemed as if the horse was close to my tent. Then it seemed that it wasn't the horse but something else. Scared, I curled up inside my sleeping bag. When the noise stopped, I had to get up, as my need to pee had turned urgent by then. When I stepped out of the tent, I saw that one of my shoes was half inside the tent and half out; I assumed it must have been the horse or some other animal who wanted to chew my shoe.

The moment I stepped out of the tent, the beauty of the sky stunned me. I had never seen so many stars; they all seemed to have come closer to the earth. The lake below seemed to be full of broken stars, surrounded by mountains awash with moonlight. I had forgotten my urge to pee in that moment. I was shivering badly in the cold, but I didn't want to return to my tent. I wanted to drink this scene, eat this view. I was thinking: If I ever wrote about this scene, would my reader be able to see what I was seeing? I knew I wasn't such a good writer.

I tried to walk towards the mountains but felt as if my entire body was hurting; I could feel extreme pain in my calves and thighs. And then I saw a human shape—I thought someone was at the bottom of the hill. But then I dismissed it thinking maybe this was some hidden fear inside me that was making me see all this. I turned and looked at the stars once more before returning to the tent; then I heaved a sigh and went inside.

In the morning I came to know that Iti's shoes were missing, and two more pairs of shoes were missing from the tent of another group. So, I had actually seen someone at night! Bilal suspected the Bakarwals and Chopans. But there were no Bakarwals around, and down below was a small settlement consisting of four huts of the Chopans. Bilal went straight to the huts of the Chopans with some people. He had assumed that someone among them might have stolen the shoes. By then, Uday and I had decided that either he or I shall give our shoes to Iti, whichever she chooses, and the other person could go downhill barefoot.

Our plan to go to Tarsar had been cancelled, and I was excited about climbing down barefoot. When all the people who had gone to look for their shoes returned empty-handed, we were sure that we would all have to return barefoot. But Bilal still hadn't come back. I was told that he had gone down towards the river to look for the shoes. After about an hour, Bilal returned with three pairs of shoes in his hands. The tent next door whooped in joy with us. Everyone gathered around Bilal to find out how and where he had found the shoes. He said someone had hidden the shoes behind a huge rock near the river.

Later, Bilal told us during breakfast, 'When I visited the Chopan homes I saw a shoe lying beside a bed and recognized that it was Iti's. The old Chopan fell to my feet and began to apologize. He put his turban on my feet. I thought that if I told people about this, they would beat him up for stealing and also burn down those four huts. So, after everyone else had gone back, I took the shoes from them and returned.'

I had seen those four Chopan huts while coming up. I was thinking about the tough life of those people at that time and how they must feel when privileged people like us pass them by, and what a tragedy it is that we also take their photographs and glorify their poverty. What exactly would they think about us at such times? Under these circumstances, how big a crime is it when an old man climbs up so far at 3 a.m. at night to steal someone's shoes? I remember reading Marx in my youth. I realize the idiocy of our discussions over chai and cigarettes in Coffee House, and then I think: Who is the thief, this old Chopan man or us?

We came down the mountain at a relaxed pace. In life, too, coming down is always easier than climbing up. On our return, we again spent the night at Green Lidderwat. My bodyache had increased, but the memories of having spent a night at the Tarsar Lake was somehow converting this pain into joy. At night we had Kashmiri food. We learnt that Bilal's family lived there. His old father came, but they didn't speak to each other. Bilal's father requested us to tell Bilal to come home; we didn't know why he was refusing to come home. Instead of him, the three of us went to his home. His father asked Iti to take a picture of their entire family, so that when he is no more, they will have this photo as a keepsake. When we returned, we showed Bilal the picture of his entire family. He became quiet looking at that picture. He showed us a hazy picture of an extremely beautiful girl in his old mobile. This was Bilal's sister, who lived with their father. About two months ago she had a severe stomach ache; by the time they took her to Anantnag she was no more.

It was nice to know that while Bilal appeared tough, he was a soft-hearted person to his core. Wiping his eyes, he said, 'I can't get this picture out of my mind. I don't go home because in the past two months my parents have aged so much that I can't bear to see them. They have completely shrivelled up. The doctors at Anantnag wanted to do my sister's post-mortem, but my father said, "Why do you want to hurt her body even more?" and began to cry. I got all the documentation done to stop the post-mortem. The doctor there looked at the papers and said, "You must have forged them." When I heard him talk like that, I picked up a chair and hit him on the head with it. I was beaten, too, by many, but I finally got my sister's body without the post-mortem.'

That night, Bilal changed for us. He had come closer to us.

It was dawn. I got up very early and went towards the deodar forests. This was my last morning in these mountains. I was full, and yet I wanted to cram these images into myself, so that on difficult days I could ponder about this morning and smile. The kids across the river had also woken up with me, and were waving at me and calling me across. I was waving at them and calling them to my side. We all stayed at our respective banks in the end. I went further into the dense deodar forest. There was a strange coolness around those trees. I rested my palm on a tree; I wanted to touch the cold. I knew this coolness; it was similar to the cold touch I had felt when I had touched my father's dead body. When I had touched him with my warm hands there was no response, only a tasteless, dead coldness.

I kept thinking about my father and Kashmir for a long time. I kept touching the trees, talking to myself loudly and listening to the loud flow of the Lidder River. That morning shall never return, that moment shall also get absorbed in the black hole of the past from which nothing ever returns. We are all travellers of a black hole in such a way that whatever we experience once never returns.

The distance I was away from Khwaja Bagh, I was the same distance away from myself and from my father too.

Is the morning over?
My hands go up again, again
To rub my three-day-old stubble
I smell the fragrance of freshly trampled new, green leaves.
I lie down. I pull my knees to my chest.
I can taste the songs of Pat Boone in my mouth.
Is it afternoon now?
Sunlight breaks through the window
Lies flat on the feet
And in the glimmer of sunlight
I feel as if they are my father's.
I have a sudden desire to pull up my feet to my chest
Instead of the knees.
An ageing atheist's body refuses to bend.

The tune of Cliff Richard's songs sails towards me from a distance
Is it evening already?

I watch the departing train for a while longer.
Father is still going towards Kashmir.
Sometimes I feel I still can
Catch the train running towards the chinars.
But I don't run. I stop.

The prickling of your beard on my cheeks
Stays with me
Like an old fragrance.

Is it night yet?

We had come to Highland Hotel in Gulmarg to have coffee. Rooh was wearing a pheran. After placing our order, we moved towards the back to sit near the *kangri*. From there, we could see patches of snow in parts of Gulmarg. Rooh had two books on Kashmir, and she was reading them one by one. I was staring at the blank screen of my laptop. When the coffee arrived, she put away the books and sipped the coffee. I saw Rooh smile for the first time since morning.

'So, tell me?'

'What?'

'We can go tomorrow.'

'Where?'

'Khwaja Bagh.'

'Why are you after it?'

'I am sure you know you have not come to Kashmir to see Gulmarg. You have come here to go there. Why are you hovering like a bee around honey?'

I was listening to her quietly. With each sip of the coffee her enthusiasm seemed to be growing.

'Okay, we'll see,' I said.

'Whether you come or not, I am booking a car for myself tomorrow. I will go to Khwaja Bagh and keep sending you pictures from there. How is that for an idea?'

I had understood that Rooh was not going to give up. After the coffee, we returned to our hotel and booked a car for the next day. I still remember that I had thanked Rooh that night. I was actually feeling very light. Had Rooh not been with me, I wouldn't have had the courage to go to Khwaja Bagh. I feared that there wouldn't be anything there. All signs must have been erased. Rooh had allayed all my fears. We were leaving at seven in the morning the next day for Khwaja Bagh.

On our way back, I was walking behind Iti and Uday; their conversations about their life together were mesmerizing, as interesting as a game of house that we played in childhood. They had been married for five years, but their conversations were as if, in Paris, they were going to live together for the first time. Closer to Aaru, on our way back, I promised them that I would visit them in Paris. I had made this promise to the Iti and Uday from my story, and to their new story that I intended to write in Paris.

As soon as I came back to the room, I opened my laptop. I did not know after how many days I was sitting in front of my novel again. I was relieved after reading a few sentences that, at least, they were still there. Sometimes, I get this strange, scary thought that I have not written the novel at all, and that it is all in my head.

When I went down after a bath, I saw a girl arguing at the counter there. She had three packed bags lying next to the counter. I just signalled to the man behind the counter that he should make my bills after resolving with her.

'Are you also checking out? Please go ahead,' the girl turned around and said to me.

'I have to leave tomorrow morning. I have time. Please go ahead and finish,' I told her.

I came out and sat on the same grass where I had been sitting before, when I had decided to go for the trek. The body was exhausted, but the mind was absolutely blank. I was trying to arrange my writing properly in my head but was unable to do so. I got up and began to roam about in the Aaru Valley. People's faces there were so amazing that I could keep looking at them for hours. Walking around, I arrived at the same chai shop where I had been the last time. This time, I sat outside as I wanted to see the people come and go. I ordered kahwa. As I looked inside the shop, I saw the same old man sitting inside the shop. He had girda and kahwa beside him. I felt like I was looking at a character that I had written and left half-written when I left for Tarsar, as if he had been waiting there for me to return from Tarsar.

'You cheated me,' he said.

'What cheating?' I said as if I didn't know him.

'I had gone to your hotel that morning. You had left for the trek.'

'Oh, yes. That was a sudden plan. I am leaving tomorrow.'

When he had finished his bread, he carried his kahwa and came outside.

'Baramulla?'

'No.'

'Then?'

'Gulmarg.'

'You are cheating again.' He laughed.

'Who?' I looked at him. His face was so similar to my father's.

'Me.'

'I don't even know you. Why would I cheat you?'

'Not knowing someone makes cheating easier. And how do you not know me? The last time we had kahwa here together. You had promised to go with me, and then you broke this promise. By those standards we know each other well.'

His words had a certain ring of mischief to them. There was so much familiar warmth in his words that nobody could be offended.

'I am actually going to Gulmarg tomorrow morning.'

'All right. So you have one more opportunity to correct your mistake.'

'What do I have to do?'

'I will take you, and you won't run away this time.'

Saying this, he extended his hand. I saw that on his wrist, just next to his thumb, was tattooed 'Mohammed'. I shook his hand, and he noticed that I was looking at the Mohammed tattoo.

'My name is Gul Mohammed. The "Gul" part has faded and is hidden by my body hair.'

He moved the white hair on his wrist, and I saw 'Gul' there.

I have met similar people with different names in my life. This was probably the first time that I met different people whose names sounded similar to me. The 'Gul Mohammed' tattooed on the old man's wrist in that chai shop seemed similar to the 'Gul Mohammed' written in my father's diary. I was amazed at how a name written in my father's diary had appeared on his arm. Am I also seeing Kashmir like I had left it? Am I unable to see Kashmir as it is in the present, now? Maybe this is the reason why, when someone wants to discuss the social or political circumstances of Kashmir, I look at them as if I have nothing to do with Kashmir. I can see only the colours of that Kashmir that is a permanent tattoo on my arm.

When I reached the hotel I was terribly hungry. I entered the kitchen. There, I saw the same girl who was arguing at the counter when I had left.

'Oh, you haven't left yet?'

'No. I shall go tomorrow morning.'

She seemed a little embarrassed about saying this. The kitchen staff was quite friendly with her. This was an indication that she had been living here for some time now. I didn't want to intervene in their conversation, so I ordered my food and went to the dining hall. In a while, she too came to the dining hall carrying her plate.

'Can I please sit with you?'

'Yes, sure.'

Her plate had cucumber, carrots, boiled spinach and a bowl of rajma.

'Your entire face is sunburnt,' she said, smiling.

'I had forgotten to apply the sunblock.'

'I have also done Tarsar Marsar recently.'

'Oh! So, while I have been here, you must have been at those heights.'

'Yes.'

'Are you travelling alone?'

'No, I was with my friends. But they wanted to return to Srinagar after Tarsar, and I am not too fond of Srinagar, hence I stayed back.'

'Srinagar is nice.'

She didn't comment on my statement.

'So where are you planning to go next?' I asked.

'I don't know. I just don't want to go back.'

'Go back to?'

'Home.'

She seemed to have a slight, tender reluctance in telling me all. While eating she got up and picked up a jug of water from another table and brought it to our table. She filled a glass of water for me and a glass for herself. I saw her properly for the first time.

'Your nose is typically Kashmiri,' I told her.

'Yes, a lot of people here also assume that I am a Kashmiri. It was only after coming here that I was told a long nose is fine. Before that I used to find my nose quite odd.'

'I am going to Gulmarg tomorrow. If you wish I can drop you somewhere.'

'Thank you. I was about to ask you the same, but I was hesitating. You might think I am imposing myself on you.'

'No, no issues at all. I will just ask my wife and tell you.'

'Wife?'

'Yes, she is sleeping upstairs.'

'All right.'

Her face had become pale. I couldn't contain my laughter. She got the joke.

'Oh God! I thought you actually have a wife, though that is not an issue.'

After the meal, I went out to the veranda for a smoke.

'Good night! I shall meet you at the counter at eight in the morning.'

She was standing on the doorstep of the hotel. In the yellow light gleaming behind her, she looked extremely beautiful. I smiled at her. There is a distinct shine in the eyes of lone travellers. Maybe that's why their sense of belonging with each other is also obvious. They think they understand the other slightly better, especially in our country, where such travellers are few in number.

'Good night,' I responded.

'By the way, my name is Roohani.'

I was slightly uncomfortable when she said that. She was gone before I could share my name. I am never expecting surprises, at least not of this kind. I thought that it is my writing that attracts such accidents. My writing finds nothing interesting in a boring person like me. Wandering alone as a lone traveller gives me great joy, but when I try to put it down in writing, I see a lot of anger in my writing. My writing is beyond my control. At each new turn, I have to change according to it. I welcome all accidents with open arms, no matter how injured I get in the process. My writing is not at all kind towards me. It pushes me into each abyss, whether I jump into it or I fall on my face, it doesn't care.

I got a call from an unknown number. The voice on the other side said, '*Beta*, how are you? I came to know that you are in Kashmir?' It was a woman's voice, full of affection.

'Ji, who's speaking?'

'Baby Aunty speaking. I got your number from your mother.'

I am running. Baby Aunty is running after me. She picks me in her lap and takes me from the stairs to her house. There, her husband, Gurpreetji, is making chicken for all of us, wearing just his underwear. Baby Aunty and I laugh for a long time looking at Gurpreetji's fat tummy.

'Where are you? How are you?'

'*Mere bachche*, we have always been here. When are you coming to Baramulla?'

'I am at Aaru Valley right now and will leave tomorrow. When I reach Khwaja Bagh I will call you.'

'Yes, son, do come. I came to know about your father's demise yesterday. It is so sad. You know, when we moved to Jammu, he came to our house, in 2010. He just knew that we lived near the roundabout. He took an auto and went from home to home around the roundabout asking, "Does Gurpreet live here?" Then a child showed him Gurpreet's house. How much he cried when he came to know that Gurpreet was no more!'

As Baby Aunty was saying this, I was trying to find Gurpreet's house in an auto with my father. The last time when he had gone to Jammu, he had even managed to find Titli.

'Yes, he had found Titli's home as well before finding you.'

'Seems like everyone is gone!'

'I will come to meet you. Where can I see you?'

'We live right beside the gurudwara that is next to the colony. You do one thing: when you reach, just call me, I will come to meet you. You just reach there.'

I was unable to say anything. My throat was choked. How much I wanted to say, 'Baby Aunty, I still love you so much! I want to hug you right now.'

When she heard only silence from my end, she said, 'Okay, beta, do call when you reach.' Then she disconnected.

After the call, I kept lying in bed for a long time. How much gets lost in a black hole and never returns! I wondered how Baby Aunty looked now. Was she still the coach of Kashmir's women badminton team? Why had she gone back to live in Khwaja Bagh? Can I also go back to Khwaja Bagh?

Why did my father keep looking for all his old neighbours? Both of us brothers had gone so far from our Kashmiriyat that he got nothing by talking to us. Mother was not Kashmiri. It was so crucial for him to touch base with those who had been around him. I understand all this now, but five years too late.

Maybe I did understand it then too, but my hypocrisy made me see only *my* story of Kashmir. How I had utilized my father and his helplessness in my play *The Man with the Yellow Scooter*. In that play, he comes to meet me, in various roles, but I am unable to meet him till the end. In the play, I didn't go out of my room. I didn't enter the emptiness of his room. How I wish he had watched my play! When I met him for the last time he had come to Bhopal. I had gone there to perform the play. He did not watch my play even then. I told him, 'Watch it. Everyone is watching my play. What would you do here all alone anyway?' He said that his knees hurt. Just like I wasn't the son he had wanted, he made every effort to not be the father I so craved for. It was impossible to say who was taking revenge on whom. But how this was affecting him and me was quite evident. While he was around, neither he changed nor I. I have not known him in my life but in my writing. That is the reason why my writings both annoy me and enamour me in equal measure. After my father passed away, I have had this desire several times—to burn all my writings.

Gul Mohammed was standing in front of the hotel—bathed, shaved, wearing new pants and a check/plaid shirt. The car was old, but going by the way it had been maintained, it seemed it was quite dear to him. Just then, Roohani also arrived with her luggage.

'I thought you were alone.'

'Yes, I was alone, but now she is with me.'

Roohani greeted him. I felt Gul didn't like her being there with us as much.

'Is he your relative?' Roohani asked as we sat in the car.

'No.'

Roohani looked at Gul surprised. He was taking us to Gulmarg via another route. We were passing by the beautiful apple valley, but my mind was still stuck with what Baby Aunty had said. Gul was talking constantly. Amid his chatter, Roohani had asked me twice if I was all right. I, too, found my behaviour quite strange. What will she think about me? What kind of a man was I? Therefore, I told her the entire story—about my birth in Khwaja Bagh and my reason for going there. Then I also told her about the call from Baby Aunty. Gul, too, was listening to this conversation.

'I had a friend: Shishir Kaul. You know, we made a separate room for him on the top of our house. Whenever he came, he stayed with us in Tangmurg. Three months ago, he died of a heart attack. By God, my entire family is grieving for him. We have left the room as it is now. Nobody has the courage to carry on with the construction any further.'

I was quietly listening to Gul's story. Such tales are quite common in the Valley. Both Hindus and Muslims have sustained these bonds of friendship with each other.

'Can I come with you to Khwaja Bagh?' Roohani asked.

'You will get bored. This is just a childhood obsession and nothing more. Maybe there is nothing even left there.'

'Don't say that. Whatever it would be I want to feel it too. If you don't have any problem?'

'Yes, do come. But whenever you get bored, feel free to go your own way.'

'All right.'

Gul had remained silent during this exchange.

'Where will you live in Gulmarg? Do you have a hotel booking?' Gul asked.

'Won't we get any kind of homestay facility? I don't like hotels,' I said.

'I have a place, if you find it convenient,' Gul said.

'She must also like it,' I said, pointing to Roohani.

'Anything is fine.'

'You will also stay with him?' Gul asked.

'Yes,' Roohani answered.

'But that is just one small room.'

'It is enough.'

'So, have you both known each other for long?' Gul asked.

'No, we just met,' Roohani replied.

'But then . . .' Gul wasn't able to complete his sentence.

'We are friends.'

I didn't interfere in that conversation between Gul and Roohani. I could sense mild anger in Roohani's voice. Gul lit a cigarette and began to look out of the car's window. A relationship of this nature was a little too much for him. So many questions of this nature were a little too much for Roohani. After a tug of war between these two different worlds, there was silence in the car.

Gul had created an image in his mind: Roohani wasn't a Kashmiri girl, she was an outsider, and everything is all right in that outside world. Now he was speaking to Roohani with ease. My conversation with her was directed more towards getting to know her better. I was not able to understand her. First, I had assumed that she was on this solo trip because of some break-up. But as soon as I said this to her, she began to laugh.

'So, this is what you assume about girls, that unless there has been a break-up in her life, a girl cannot be on a solo trip?'

'I am sorry, but I was trying to . . .'

'To?'

'To know why you are travelling alone?'

She came close to me and whispered into my ear in English, 'There is not much of a difference between you and our driver.'

I apologized again. 'Achha, then you tell me yourself,' I almost pleaded.

'I just don't want to go back to Mumbai right now. Just that.'

We had crossed Tangmurg and were now climbing towards Gulmarg. We were surrounded by a dense deodar forest. It had become slightly cold. This was where I could smell Kashmir for the first time.

'Did you notice the air here is different. Inhale its fragrance.'

Roohani opened the car window on her side fully. I couldn't tell her that this was the fragrance of Kashmir. 'This is the fragrance of the mountains that I am quite fond of.'

She closed her eyes and inhaled. Her hair was flying in the wind, and there was a beautiful smile on her face. I, too, began to look outside. Baramulla was just one and a half hours away from here. I was very close. On the way I saw several road signs with 'Baramulla' written on them and an arrow marking the direction. I was not headed there, but I was close, and I was happy about that. I began to see the white walls and blue door of the Khwaja Bagh home. There was snow in the front yard, and the sun was shining on the walls of the house.

'Would you give me a neck-and-shoulder massage?' Roohani asked.

'Yes, my calves are aching a lot too. In return you will have to put your legs on them.'

'Calves, what's that?' (She hadn't got the Hindi word for it.) She had asked this with extreme simplicity. I laughed and pointed at my calves.

'Oh, I was wondering!'

'What did you think?'

There was the slightest hint of flirtation from both our ends. She smiled. Then she slowly came close to me and said, 'Listen, we won't have sex.'

As she said this, a mischievous smile spread on her face. I was a little scared as I thought Gul must have heard this.

He looked at us once in the rear-view mirror and then lit a cigarette.

'Why are you blushing?' Roohani asked.

'I wasn't ready for this.'

'For what?'

'Let it go.'

When we reached Gulmarg we realized that everyone knew Gul Mohammed. We had to stop at least fifteen times while going towards his shop. With so many greetings exchanged, it was evident to me that Gul was an old-timer around here. His shop had 'Gul Skiing Adventure' written on it. There was a staircase on the side that led to the small room on top.

'I live in this room,' he said as we reached the room.

'Then where will you stay?' Roohani asked.

'I live here in the winter. At this time of the year, I shall go to my home in Tangmurg.'

The entire room was stocked with skiing and winter sports equipment. There were mattresses and quilts in one corner.

'I had assumed that you would be alone, but now that you are two people, let me get another mattress laid out.'

'No, let it be. We can manage on one mattress,' Roohani said, and Gul looked a bit embarrassed.

'So, both of you can rest. I shall go downstairs to the shop.'

Before going, Gul looked once at Roohani as if he was looking at an alien. Then he went down clearing his throat. We were both waiting for him to leave.

'What is his problem with me?' Roohani said as soon as Gul left.

'You tell me if this room is okay for you, or else we can go to a hotel.'

'Then this gentleman will say girls can't live in rooms like this one.'

'Forget about him. You tell me, is this room okay?'

'Absolutely. Come what may, I will stay here.'

Roohani and I took up the responsibility of making that room liveable. She shook the mattress; I made a pile of the quilts in one corner, and we arranged all the equipment in one part of the room properly. Now the room looked a bit liveable. I brought chai from downstairs. The door and windows of the room were in a row, and the windows had glass panes. There was no curtain, so anyone coming up could peep into the room from the windows before reaching the door. I had also noticed that the door of the room could not be shut—its hinges were broken.

'Why are you wrestling with the door? Who would come here?' Roohani said. And I let the door be. There was a small space outside the door that could be called an open balcony. I put a mattress and a pillow there, and began to work on my laptop. Roohani took a violin out of her bag and sat next to me.

'Won't you get disturbed?'

'If you play well, I might write better.'

'I am just practising.'

'I am also just trying to write.'

'Okay then, let's see.'

She slowly tuned the violin and began to play some notes softly. I was writing, but my ears were focused on the notes of the violin. The entire Gulmarg was visible from that balcony.

'O! The girl is talented too,' Gul said, peeping from the side of his shop downstairs. Roohani stopped playing.

'Please play, it sounds nice,' he said, but by then it was too late.

'I am going to rest inside.' Roohani smiled once at Gul and went into the room.

I began to write on my laptop, in the absence of the notes of the violin.

We had walked to, and were strolling in, the quieter forests of Gulmarg. There was snow on the ground, but sunshine was filtering through the trees and touching our bodies; hence we weren't feeling as cold.

'Can I read something out to you?' Rooh had asked.

'Yes, read.' I hadn't spoken a word for so long that I had to clear my throat to say this. Rooh stood under a deodar tree. I leant against the same tree. Everything around the deodar trees was white, and with every word Rooh's breath condensed into vapour.

'This is Lal Ded, whom I admire a lot:

Who is to die and who can they kill?
Who can kill and who is to die?
One who gorges God for the sake of the hearth,
Is sure to die and is to be killed.'

'Really nice,' I said.

'I like history a lot. Roaming in old forts, I feel as if, just yesterday, a king must have stepped out to meet his queen. Or from here, he must have declared war, from there the soldiers must have rushed in,' Rooh said.

'Yes, it is fascinating to walk through empty forts.'

'You know, in every country and every religion there have been people like Lal Ded, who have beautifully spoken about brotherhood, mutual love and peace, and they have been quite popular among the commoners too, and yet this hatred has not decreased.'

'I think people get bored. Like, in our country, people have become bored of Gandhi. Whenever someone mentions something else except non-violence about Gandhi, everyone becomes cautious. We constantly need drama in our lives. Look at our homes, for instance. Even among four–five family members we create so much drama that it becomes almost impossible to survive with each other.'

'It is not that simple,' Rooh said, and she began to walk upwards on the mountain in the snow. I wanted to click her picture at that moment. Walking in snow with the dense deodar forest around her, she looked like a painting.

'What does that mean?' I asked and didn't take that picture. Rooh didn't like to be photographed. In any case, how could one click Rooh?

'In 1947, there was a slogan—"*Sher-e-Kashmir, kya irshaad! Hindu, Muslim, Sikh itehaad* (Lions of Kashmir, what do you say! Hindu, Muslim and Sikh unity)." It had led to peace in the Valley. Then, in 1990, a similar-sounding slogan spread—"*People's League ka kya paigam? Fateh, aazadi aur Islam* (What is the message of the People's League? Victory, freedom and Islam)." These frivolous rhymes play a crucial role in dividing people. These are like cheap songs that get on to your tongue; whether you like them or not, you find yourself humming them. Lal Ded is quite famous, but she can never compete with these frivolous trends. And now, social media further adds fuel to the fire of these rhyming trends. The countries where people don't understand good poetry and good music are prone to more violence.'

'Do you think being very pretty is also a curse?' I asked.

'Yes, every person wants to rip off and consume their share of the beauty.'

We kept discussing beauty for long, and every conversation would route back to Kashmir.

'Will you ever come again to Kashmir, on your own . . .?'

'I don't know. Listen, would you take a picture?' Rooh asked.

'Yours? You don't like being clicked. Otherwise this has been on my mind for some time now.'

'I know that. Your hand was going to your phone again and again. Not mine but of this jungle. I want to save this picture and keep it with me. This is real Kashmir to me.'

I gave Rooh my phone, and she took a picture of her Kashmir. I had begun to think about my Kashmir at that point. If I had to click just one picture of Kashmir, which one would it be? I kept thinking about it for a long time but had no conclusive answer.

The sun was quite strong, and I was writing about snow. I looked inside the room where Roohani was sleeping. I closed my laptop and lay down beside her.

'You forgot your promise?'

She was facing the wall; she pointed at her shoulder. I began to massage around her shoulder and neck.

'Your massage is just like your singing.' Roohani was laughing.

'When did you hear me sing?'

'You were continuously humming in the car.'

'That means I am massaging badly.'

'When did I say that?'

'This is not how massage is done. One needs oil. There has to be music and the entire atmosphere for it.'

'But even then, if you don't get your notes right . . .'

'Then I would agree that I sing badly.'

Roohani played a beautiful song by Keith Jarret on her mobile and handed me a bottle of oil. She had bought this almond oil in Kashmir. Before lying down she removed her kurti. She was wearing a sports bra underneath it. By the time I had put some oil in my hands she had removed the sports bra as well. Hesitating, I looked at my hands; they were shaking. The moment I touched Roohani I felt as if she was not there and I was alone in the room. Am I actually there? Am I writing this or living this? We both could play this massage game briefly. We had both undressed. Roohani put her hands on my chest and pushed me back a little. She looked at me naked, intently, from tip to toe. I felt shy and hid from her. We were giggling.

We had just begun to explore each other's bodies on that narrow bed when I heard a noise. By the time I could comprehend I saw a man working in Gul's shop just outside the window. He was about to enter the room when I shouted. Roohani started laughing at my shouting. By that time the man had opened the door and entered the room. Roohani was laughing continuously, and I was trying to pull up the quilt. I quickly threw the quilt over her body. The man stood shocked at the door for a few moments; he then turned around and ran back downstairs.

'There was a smile on his face. Did you see?' Roohani said laughing.

I had also seen him smile just before he left.

'Did he see everything?' I asked.

'What's everything?' Roohani was still laughing. I wore my clothes and went straight to Gul's shop. Gul was having his meal; that man was also there.

'Do you need anything?' Gul asked.

'No,' I said, looking at that man.

'So?' Gul asked.

'We want to rest for a while. So nobody should come upstairs.'

Gul said, 'Yes, sure. Please rest.'

I was surprised that the man's face was expressionless, as if he had not come upstairs at all. I wanted to tell him, 'You are a brilliant actor, my friend.' But I came out from there embarrassed. Roohani was still laughing. She dragged me to the bed again. While removing my clothes I was telling Roohani what had happened downstairs in the shop. We were both in bed again, and we were both laughing. But time and again, I felt as if someone would come up to the window and peep in. I stopped Roohani and began to look for a bedsheet in Gul's junk.

'What are you doing. Please come,' said Roohani.

'Let me put a curtain on that window first.'

I couldn't find a bedsheet, but there was a large, thick piece of cloth. As I shook and straightened it, I felt something getting stuck to my penis. I saw that a glue pad, used to trap mice, was stuck on my penis. I screamed. I managed to get that pad off, but a lot of glue remained stuck on my penis. Just then, I noticed that Gul had scattered a lot of those pads all around the room. Roohani had been continuously laughing for the last half hour, and now she was teary-eyed because of it. I picked up a towel and ran straight to the bathroom. It took me about an hour to get all the glue off my body. As soon as I came out I heard Roohani shout. When I rushed upstairs I saw her shivering in a corner.

'What happened?'

'The mouse was in my bag. The moment I opened it, it jumped on me.'

I understood it would be difficult to stay there. I went downstairs and told Gul, 'We need a hotel immediately.'

In an hour we were in a clean room in a hotel.

Gul Mohammed had come to our hotel early in the morning, and we had finished our breakfast.

'Let me take you to a new place today,' he said, sitting on our table.

'Where?' Roohani asked.

'Tosa Maidan was under army occupation till 2014 but is now open to the general public. It is an amazing place.'

'Shall we go in the evening?' Roohani asked.

'We shall be able to come back by evening. It is a four-hour-long drive. We have to start now. My shabby old car moves slowly.'

Roohani and I kept looking at each other.

In almost an hour or so we were in his car, having set out for Tosa Maidan. The road was all right for the first two hours, but after that it was an unpaved road. Roohani was sitting in front, and I was in the back. The entire car was filled with dust. Neither Roohani nor I liked this journey. But just to avoid saying this to Gul Mohammed we were both saying nice things about the journey.

'By when shall we reach?' asked Roohani.

'Just half an hour more.'

'There was an army presence here. Was anything wrong here?'

'No, this area was used for artillery practice. Nothing is wrong now anywhere in Kashmir,' Gul said smilingly.

'The news that reaches outside is dreadful.'

'Things are as bad here as they are in other places, but it is easy to
stir the sentiments of people—both in India and in Pakistan. Hence
it is easy to use it for that.'

'Have you ever seen a terrorist?'

'You are sitting with one right now.'

Roohani suddenly turned around and looked at me. I was sitting
quietly and listening to both of them. Suddenly, there was slight fear
in Roohani's eyes. When she realized that I would not be able to help
much, she asked in fear, 'Are you telling the truth?'

'Yes. You tell me who is a terrorist? The image you have in your
mind is not me. Here we call them freedom fighters. If they do
something wrong, loot someone or kill the local people, then they
are actually terrorists. We are not them.'

There was silence in the car after that. But I couldn't resist any
more. I raised questions about the JKLF and Hizbul. When I spoke
about their internal conflicts and their aim of making Kashmir an
Islamic state, he became a little hesitant. 'I don't know anything
about these people.'

Kashmir accepts rumours as news. We witnessed this during
COVID in the entire country too. Once rumour begins, social media
fans the fire, and it spreads like wildfire in a jungle. Gul Mohammed
knew that I was writing something about Kashmir; so he would be
extra cautious while talking to me. He had a different equation with
Roohani. He liked scaring her.

'I was saying it just like that, beta,' Gul said to Roohani.

'You actually scared me,' Roohani said.

'You don't need to be scared of anyone. People here are
very good.'

Then the conversation turned towards goodness. The
atmosphere in the car became lighter as we reached Tosa Maidan.
It was very beautiful; one could see the expanse of green mountains
from there. It seemed as if there could be many golf courses here.
Maybe the tiredness of the Tarsar track had still not left Roohani's
body and mine, hence we weren't liking this place as much. After

having a meal in Tosa Maidan, we came down the same bad road. By the time we returned to Gulmarg it was almost evening.

'Now tell me. When do you want to go to Khwaja Bagh?' Gul asked on the way to dropping us at our hotel.

'Not tomorrow. I will tell you,' I said.

'You didn't enjoy Tosa Maidan.'

'No, that's not true. It was quite nice,' Roohani answered.

Gul must've been close to seventy. I could always sense the fatigue of the responsibility of Kashmir in his body. He wanted people to see Kashmir from the point of view of Kashmiris. I liked this about him a lot. But Kashmir is so deeply entrenched in its issues and history that even trivial questions can trigger trauma. We urban people are in the habit of hiding our trauma, but Kashmir is full of open wounds. It is a man's own story—his lived trauma and the fatigue it brings. On top of that an emotional Kashmiri like me arrives, who only has the happy images of his childhood; and in addition to this he wants to write about Kashmir as well . . . All these facts lead to new paradoxes. I myself struggle with it. Often I don't want to know too much about Kashmir. I remain quiet about my questions. But the moment I mention that I am a Pandit and I was born here, my hiding space ceases to be. I have to speak and listen. I never understood Islamic Kashmir or the Kashmir of the Pandits; for me, Kashmir belongs to Sufism and Shaivism, and it is heartening that even today one finds some signs of both scattered here and there in Kashmir.

'I need a drink,' Roohani said and collapsed on the bed.

'There is one hotel here that serves alcohol.'

'I won't step out of this room now.'

'It will be difficult to get a drink here in the room.'

Roohani had wrapped herself in the quilts; I had opened my laptop and had begun to work on my novel.

In Gulmarg, we were having extremely lazy days. I would wake up at five in the morning and work; and then at around seven I would wake Roohani up with loads of kisses and cuddles, and then go for a walk with her. We would go looking for a *kandur** about three kilometres away, buy some lavas and girda from there, and then go to a small dhaba. Roohani would then have kahwa there and I would have noon chai. On our way back, we would almost always find a local with whom I would strike a conversation. Roohani loved the hotel balcony. Whenever I would sit with my laptop to write, she would play the violin on the balcony. The notes of her violin could be found in my Kashmiri writings.

'Would you find it strange if I say thanks to you?' I asked.

'Your manner of saying thanks is quite strange.'

'So, how should I thank you?'

She put my laptop away on the table and took me to bed.

I would take Roohani to the same dhaba where Rooh and I used to go every day. I recognized Firoz, who worked there; but he probably didn't recognize me. I didn't have a beard earlier. Eating rajma chawal at the shop I was thinking, Was I able to thank Rooh? Maybe not. Had it not been for her, I wouldn't have known Kashmir even as little as I do now.

---

* Bakery where one finds fresh local breads, etc.

'**D**on't you feel angry? I find this strange,' Rooh had said once while we were walking.

We were used to eating in small shops. Neither she nor I liked the food at the bigger hotels. Walking across the snow on the sides of the road, we would often reach Firoz's small shop via smaller paths. Their most frequent customers were tonga owners and drivers. No matter how much one ate, the bill was always so little that Rooh would be surprised. The food was always too spicy for Rooh, but she would never ask for the quantity of chillies to be reduced. She would always step out from there wiping her watery eyes.

'What would I achieve by being angry?' I said.

'But you could have at least said something.'

'You can speak too.'

'I wish my Hindi was good.'

She was right. Had her Hindi been good, no man could ever have a conversation with her. She remembered all the books she had read in sequence.

'Now I feel I should have spoken. But you know, I am never able to remember incidents and their dates.'

'You don't have to win a quiz competition. You can at least talk about your father's experiences,' she said.

'I find it slightly hypocritical.'

'In Pahalgam, Srinagar and Gulmarg, everyone just knows that the Pandits had run away. Don't you know that running away and being chased away is not the same thing? And how did this rumour spread? How do you find this hypocritical? How? I don't understand.'

'I am living an extremely good life. These people are here. And the entire world makes up history as per its convenience. The more you argue, the angrier they become, because nobody wants to be proven wrong. Had my father been here, he probably would have explained all of this properly in Kashmiri, but as far as I know, my father probably wouldn't have been able to explain it. He would have become angry, just like you.'

'Maybe you are right. I have met people in America who believe that the earth is not round, or that the Holocaust was a hoax. Just like you, I too become surprisingly quiet in front of such people.'

'Actually, there are multiple truths.'

'Because lies are repeated, they start sounding like the truth.'

'But who knows what the truth actually sounds like?'

'This nobody can ever know.'

'That is why I keep saying often that I am a good man.'

Rooh laughed a lot when I said this.

'Do you know that in 1992, there were two people named Sunil Kaul and Sumesh Bhan, who had planned to bomb a school? But the bomb burst in Sunil's hands, and he died on the spot, and Sumesh was badly injured.'

'How do you know this?'

'All the Kashmiris living in Jammu had condemned this incident and any kind of violence on social media.'

'I didn't know about this at all.'

We were both feeling quite cold after the meal. Though our original plan was to go for a long walk, we headed back to the hotel instead.

'We are going to Khwaja Bagh tomorrow,' Rooh said as we reached near the hotel.

'I know that you have booked the car. By the way, do you know how Khwaja Bagh came to be known as Khwaja Bagh?' I changed the topic.

'No. Please tell me.' Rooh helped me by saying that.

'Not facts, but just hearsay. Its name is Khwaja Bagh, and it means Garden of the Rich. Before Independence the road used for trade between India and Pakistan passed through Varmul or Baramulla. So, Baramulla was an important town, and Khwaja Bagh was the residential area of rich people.'

'Good. At least you were born in a rich place. Whether you remained rich or not later is a different issue.'

'There are many issues. Good that you booked a car for tomorrow. I was wondering how to go.' Rooh was very close to me.

'I am very close to you.'

'I am feeling extremely cold today.'

'It isn't the cold but the dampness inside you.'

That night I pulled Rooh very close to me. I wanted to sleep in her warmth.

We asked Gul Mohammed about alcohol, and he said that there was only one shop in Srinagar that opened only thrice a week, or we would have to go to the only hotel in Gulmarg. But Roohani didn't want to leave the room, so I called a friend of mine who is in the army. He said that he would make some arrangements in an hour. After an hour he informed us that we would have to go to this particular army cantonment and fetch the alcohol; he had given the necessary instructions to a jawan. We were happy. I called that army jawan immediately, and he asked me to come around 8 p.m. for the pick-up. Roohani said that we could not take Gul along for this. So we spoke to a local driver, who agreed to do the trip with us. He came to pick us up precisely at 8 p.m., but when we asked him to take us to the army camp, he was slightly hesitant. Only when I told him that I would pay him more did he agree to go. But the moment we got closer to the army camp the driver got scared again: 'Listen, I shall drop you here only. I will not enter the army camp.'

'You don't have to worry. I have already spoken to an army officer inside. Please come along.'

He was driving so slowly that from a distance anyone would have found it suspicious.

'My friend, please move ahead. Why are you so scared?'

'Sir, they are the army. They can do anything.'

'You stop the car here. Let me have a word with the jawan.'

I was scared that the sentry could start questioning the driver. Hence I got down from the car and spoke to the sentry. There we came to know that we had to go to gate number three. So I sat in the car again.

'Let's go inside,' I said.

'How can we go inside? Isn't it prohibited?'

'I have just spoken to them. We are with you.'

He moved the car ahead slowly. I noticed that he was constantly mumbling something, '*Auzu billahi minash shaitan rajeem . . .*'

The moment he saw an army vehicle coming towards us from the opposite side, he halted his car. We had just reached the second gate, but he stopped the car and said, 'I won't go any further, and I do not want to be either a friend or an enemy of the army people. You can go ahead beyond this point. Anything can happen there.'

I was about to say something to the driver, but Roohani spoke to the driver instead. 'It is really dark up ahead. How will we go on foot? Please take us, and tomorrow we also have to go to Baramulla. If you take us to gate three today, we will take your car for Baramulla tomorrow as well.'

He agreed to Roohani's offer and moved the car ahead, but he was loudly chanting, 'Auzu billahi minash shaitan rajeem . . .'

I got down at the third gate, went inside and got the bottle of rum. The driver reversed the car quickly, and as soon as we were out of the army camp, he parked the car on the side and peed. When he came back his breathing had returned to normal.

'You have some good contacts. You got alcohol from the army people,' the driver said.

'They are also humans, and they are also good people, just like the Kashmiris,' Roohani said.

'What are you saying?' the driver exclaimed.

'Just like you risk your life for livelihood, they too . . .' said Roohani.

'So, when do you want to start for Baramulla?'

'You come at seven in the morning. We shall be there,' I told him, paid his fare and alighted. Roohani was excited about the rum. As soon as we reached the room, she added some honey to hot water, made two pegs of rum and handed one to me.

'Cheers to Khwaja Bagh!'

I said cheers and sat on the balcony with my drink.

'You don't seem excited.'

'Ever since Baby Aunty called me, all I want is to return to Khwaja Bagh. I don't know why I have this strange habit that wherever I want to go desperately, I also nurture a fear of going there.'

'What's the fear?'

'That there would be nothing there.'

'You are again thinking the same way.'

'I know the white walls and blue door of my home are still there. I feel reassured due to this. More than me, my dreams are sure of this. But if there is nothing there, then understand that Khwaja Bagh would be wiped out from all my future dreams.'

'I feel you need to touch it for real more than in dreams.'

'Baby Aunty belonged to Patiala.' I tried to change the topic. 'She had trained in badminton there. When she came to Khwaja Bagh, she appeared in the interview for a coach. But they had appointed some local Kashmiri as the coach in Khwaja Bagh. Baby Aunty went to the court. They had to finally remove the other person and appoint her as the coach. Her women's badminton team would lose at most places that they went to. If anyone asked Baby Aunty about it, she would say, "What if we lose? The crowd only gathers to watch Kashmiri girls play."'

'Whenever you speak about Baby Aunty it seems you are talking about your mother.'

'My brother and I are just a year apart. It was Baby Aunty in whose lap I played. She would never let me out of sight. She has two sons, but nobody else got the love that I did. I can still feel her hands on my body.'

'Shouldn't you tell her that you are going there?'

'I will send a message.'

'Make a call.'

'I wouldn't be able to control myself after listening to her voice.'

'All right, send a message then.'

As soon as I messaged, I got her reply: 'Come, beta, I am here.' I kept seeing myself running in the colony for hours. Using a curtain to play in my friend Kaka's home, hovering over Titli, waiting for a tonga during winters and, during all this, the stress of India–Pakistan cricket matches. Whenever there were these matches, the environment at home and in the colony used to be quite charged. The radio would be kept in the middle of the room, and my father and his friends would sit surrounding it. The room would be full of cigarette smoke and rounds of tea would continue. If Pakistan won the match, as was common in those days, my father would smash the radio on the wall in the end. I don't remember how many radios have been martyred in these matches. All friends would curse the Indian team generously. After the match, Father would jump out of the window, lock the door of the house from outside and then return and sit inside. He would not go to the office as well for two–three days. If India won, father and his friends would bathe and dress up, and then step out and distribute sweets in the entire colony. The colony had an equal number of supporters of the Indian and Pakistani teams. Yet if the situation ever heated up at the border, one would witness the fighter planes in the sky above Khwaja Bagh. The lights would be out then, and not even candles were allowed. In this darkness, Father would often tell stories of war. I don't remember those stories, but I remember their sense of secrecy even today. Often, in such a situation, I would ask my father, 'Where would we go if there is a war?'

'We shall fight. For our people,' he would whisper.

'Our people?' I would ask.

'I will fight for Gul Mohammad; you fight for your friends.'

'But he supports the Pakistani team?' I was too young at that time and did not understand the seriousness of these questions.

'So what! It's no fun watching a match without that too.'

I began to think about my dream again, where I was in Khwaja Bagh but unable to go to my house. I was looking towards the house, but I couldn't see the blue door and white walls. Maybe this time my reluctance to go to Khwaja Bagh stemmed from this dream. I always believed that one evolves constantly; all new literature that you read changes you; the films that you watch and the journeys that you take change you. But some lived experiences, especially those of childhood, stay deposited like heavy rocks at the bottom of the river of life—they don't change due to any flood or storm in life. Then, whenever you dive deep into the river, you find all those rocks there as it is, as if they were waiting for you to dive in.

While writing this almost imaginary travelogue I had never imagined that Kashmir was causing such turmoil inside me. I opened my Instagram and looked for Rooh's account. She had recently married an American boy. I was very happy to see her wedding pictures. She was smiling in all her pictures. I wanted to congratulate her and tell her that I was in Kashmir and I was writing. I wrote a comment on one of her pictures, 'Congratulations to you, Rooh!'

When Rooh and I were going to Khwaja Bagh the driver asked, 'Is madam a foreigner?'

'Yes, she is from America,' I answered.

'The situation here is not nice, especially for foreigners. They need special permission to visit.'

'We didn't know.'

'But she looks like an Indian. You ask her to cover her head, and if a police or army vehicle stops us, stay quiet.'

When I said this to Rooh, instead of becoming scared she was excited. She covered her head with a scarf.

'Now you are looking like a Kashmiri,' the driver said smilingly. I wanted her to be scared. My fear was different. Had she been scared too, then in sympathizing with her I might have allayed my fears for some time at least.

'We are about to reach Khwaja Bagh. You remember where your home was?'

There was a big colony gate and another gate on its side, which was the gate of the office of Dipper Dredge, where my father worked. I had seen all this about three decades ago. But I was sure that when we crossed the colony gate, I would instantly recognize it.

'Yes, I know. You keep driving.'

115

I was looking out of the window. Rows of tall eucalyptus trees were moving with us on the sides of the road. I recognized those trees. So many times, while coming from Srinagar to Khwaja Bagh, sitting in my father's lap, I would see those trees from the bus window. The moment Father would see these trees he would say, 'Now, we are closer to home.'

'*Bhai*, we have crossed Khwaja Bagh,' the driver said.

'What? When?'

'We have come further ahead, Baramulla up ahead.'

'So, stop the car, turn around. How could I not have seen the colony gate? How can this be?'

'Never mind. We shall turn around and tell him to drive slowly.' Rooh put her hands on my shoulder and head.

I was constantly looking out of the window, and I was anxious that whatever I had remembered from my childhood was all untrue. We returned at a slower speed.

'Just stop where the buses drop people for Khwaja Bagh,' I told the driver.

'Yes, sir.'

He answered as if he had got a whiff of my untrue childhood. I didn't make eye contact with him. I was constantly looking out. One glimpse, just an old memory, one sign—I hoped to see something, but I couldn't find anything with which I could show that I was not lying. Just then, the driver stopped the car saying, 'So, this is Khwaja Bagh. Tell me, where was your house?'

I got out of the car and began to look around. I went to a shop there and asked, 'Bhai, there used to be a Dipper Dredge colony here. Where is that?'

'Is it behind that wall?'

I turned around and there was a wall.

'But there used to be a gate here.'

'After the earthquake of 2005 they removed the gate and erected this wall.'

Just then I saw the tin roof of the houses behind the wall. I don't know how, but I recognized all those tin roofs.

'You can enter that colony from the rear end of the lane.'

I ran to Rooh. She was sitting in the car with her head covered.

'The colony is across the gate, which we used to escape after stealing apples. It is through which we will have to enter now.'

Rooh didn't understand but the driver did. He turned the car into that lane. The moment we reached in front of the door I patted the driver's seat. 'Stop, just stop here. This is my home.'

I noticed that Rooh had been holding my hand throughout.

'Shall we go?' I asked her.

'You go ahead. I will follow,' she said.

She wanted me to enter alone. I got off the car and stepped inside through the big, broken gate. The first spot inside was the ground that still had the three-decade-old iron rods. As I moved further, I saw the lane, at the end of which our home used to be. But in my dreams, everything had been huge. The ground was actually quite small. The lane of our house was short.

'Why is this entire colony empty?' Rooh called out from behind.

'I don't know.'

The colony was empty, and the houses dilapidated and barely holding up. The lane leading to my home was full of sludge. I walked through the sludge and reached the end, and I could see: a broken blue door and the almost white cracked walls. This house, too, was so small. In my dreams it had been as tall as a deodar. In reality, it was an ordinary house in an average government colony. I climbed the stairs and stood in the small veranda of the house. The door was broken, and I was peeping inside as if I wanted permission from someone to enter. There was dead silence inside. I didn't have the courage to touch the door. I took the phone from my pocket and called my father, 'Hello, Papa! I am standing at the door of our home in Khwaja Bagh.'

There was silence for a few moments, and then he said, 'Where?'

I repeated. He again remained quiet for some time and then said, 'How is the house?'

'It is very nice. It is small but nice.'

'Here, speak to your mother.'

There was antiquity in his voice. It matched the house in Khwaja Bagh. I didn't wish to speak with my mother at that point, so I disconnected the call after a while. I didn't understand why Father didn't want to speak to me, and I didn't ask him this.

I pushed the door reluctantly. After a few minutes of struggle the door finally opened. Stepping into the house was completely like stepping into the past. Maybe nobody else had even lived in this space in all these years. Sitting room, the window of the sitting room, the room with the bukhari, where all of us slept in a row during winters. Darkened kitchen walls. Bathroom and storeroom towards the back . . . Rooh was standing outside the house. I took out my phone and took a picture of the window in the bukhari room. This window was very important for me. Sitting here in winters, I would see the smoke rise from the bukhari rooms of other homes. This was where I had learnt to stare at the sky for hours. I would lose awareness of how the changing forms of rabbits and elephants in the white clouds against the blue sky would transform into stories. My friend Kaka's house was right across. Just then, I remembered where I used to hide toffees. I went to the wall of the main door of my house and saw that that part was perfectly fine. I put my finger into that cavity—my finger that was thicker now—and then I lost all control. I couldn't understand why I was crying. For whom? I couldn't stay in that house any longer and stepped outside.

I was about to walk out of the colony when I saw a woman peeping down from the second floor of an adjacent home in the lane. She called out, 'Who are you looking for?'

I said as loudly as I could, 'I am from here. I was born in that last house, there at the end of the lane.' Maybe the last few words hadn't come out of my throat.

'Okay.'

'Kaka lived on the ground floor. He used to be my friend. Does he still live here?'

'Yes, he is about to be a father. Hence they are all in Srinagar. They will be back in two–three days.'

I was surprised to know that Kaka was still here. There was so much I wanted to ask the woman, but my legs felt lifeless. I was unable to stand. I told Rooh that we must leave.

'Stay for a while more. You don't know if you will ever be able to come here again,' Rooh said.

'I will come, but right now I can't stay here.'

I saw that my father was calling me, but I disconnected the call.

This was six years ago. In the meantime, my father passed away. The only picture that I had clicked of the window of the bukhari room, I used it as the cover of my first short-story collection, *Theek Tumhare Peechhe* (Right Behind You). Earlier, I used to dream of the whole house of Khwaja Bagh. Now even in my dreams the house appeared broken. I had become busy, but again and again I was reminded that Rooh had asked me to stay a bit longer, but I wasn't able to. I always knew that I would come to Kashmir and spend some days in this colony. But between writing and travelling the promises I'd made to my Rooh had faded. Then COVID took away two years. Now, after six years, I was in Kashmir again.

I hadn't been able to write about him, because I hadn't got their consent. Somehow, I got connected to him again, and I sought his consent that I wanted to put our conversation in my book. He had said that two years ago he would have said no to it, but now he didn't care.

I had met him during my stay in Srinagar. His name was Jeevan. A Kashmiri Pandit, white-bearded, tall man, whose voice had the peculiar rasp of a chain-smoker. When I would take my small boat to the middle of the lake, he could be seen sitting near the window of the adjacent houseboat with his laptop. I would imagine he must be a writer writing diligently. I would often snub the writer in me by comparing myself with him. Why didn't I have the same stillness? Because I wanted to get away from my laptop after a bit of writing.

One day, he was strolling on the deck of his houseboat. I was anchoring my small boat when I heard him ask from there, 'Do you have a lighter?' He had asked this in Kashmiri. I understood the word 'lighter' and said yes.

'Wait. I will come down.'

'No, I will come.' After saying this I went to his houseboat. Taking the lighter from me, he said, 'You are a Kashmiri.'

'Yes.'

'I could make out just by looking at you. Would you like some tea?' Before I could give my consent he had ordered two cups of tea.

Jeevan was born in Batmaloo, Kashmir, in 1962. I asked Jeevan about where he lived currently, and he just shrugged. The light banter around tea soon turned into a conversation about serious issues of Kashmir.

'Yesterday, I was with Usman. Had you met me yesterday, you would have had a lot of fun.'

'Usman?' My eyes popped out in surprise. I understood which Usman he was talking about.

'Yes.'

'Do you know him?'

'Yes,' he said with ease. 'I met him for the first time about twenty years ago. Now I don't remember the precise details. We had met via a back channel in some hotel in Panchgani. Many people from India and Pakistan were present in that meeting. I remember, even Ahmed Faraz was present at that meeting. I had somehow made arrangements for alcohol in the evening. I told Usman, "Let's go and have a couple of drinks." He said, "See, we are discussing Kashmir, and this conversation could be crucial. If we stink of alcohol during that, it won't look good." I was so impressed by him for this, and we became good friends after that. He was educated and had gone to the other side for training. Meaning he had become so good that the Pakistani commandos had made him in charge of a training camp, and he was now training other Kashmiris.'

'How did Usman experience a change of heart?' I asked.

'It is said that one night a Pakistani general invited him for drinks. Usually, Pakistani generals kept a safe distance from Kashmiris, but Usman was different. After a few pegs, when the conversation became freewheeling, Usman said, "Sir, as far as I remember, about forty of your groups are active in Kashmir. If we combine all those groups into one, how much more effective we would be?" The general agreed with Usman. Then Usman asked, "So, why don't you bring them all under one roof?" The general said, finishing his peg, "Because we don't trust you people." Usman said that the general had accidentally said this. But after returning to Kashmir, he could not forget it. Here, when he was given some operations to complete, he realized that he was killing his own people. He realized that it was all happening at the instructions from the other side. They decided whom to take out, whom to promote, and those being killed were all Kashmiris. In all of this, he felt that even he would be next on that list. Then he picked up arms against all terrorists. Usman, Liyaqat, Kukumure and a Kashmiri Pandit were also part of this. Kukumure was their head and was killed later. People called them "Ikhwan" and used to be peeved with them. They eradicated the terrorists from many villages. They got full support from India. Usman was an inside man and had trained many of these people. Hence he knew it all.'

'Usman should have been India's hero in a way.'

'Definitely. He used to say that India is making Yaseen Malik a hero; rather, they should make him the hero, so that Kashmiris who go across to get trained come to know what those on the other side think about us.'

Our chai was finished. He lit cigarettes for both of us, and we came down on the houseboat. 'Let's go and walk towards the back. I hope you don't have anything to attend to.'

'No. I wait for these moments only.'

'What do you mean?'

'I mean I find unplanned relationships like this one quite charming.'

'So, are you going to write about all this?'

'Not without your consent.'

'Then it is all right.'

He had neither agreed nor refused at that point. We walked towards the back.

'You are a Pandit. How do you feel here now?'

'My friend, you see, whatever I say doesn't please the Pandits much. We are now irrelevant. Our vote percentage is dismal.

Yes, there is pain inside Pandits, which is valid. But then, many years have also passed since then. Now I will tell you something. We Pandits were less than ten per cent and were in a way ruling the rest of the ninety per cent people. This means all the power, land, respect, jobs were ours, and on top of that we were insensitive. The Muslim milk vendor's vessel must not touch ours when he comes for delivering the milk. The servant at home is a Muslim, but he can't enter the kitchen. In a tonga, if a Pandit was already seated, a Muslim could not sit next to him. When we met a Pandit on the way we called him Mehra, and when we saw a Muslim, we would say something derogatory. So, whatever happened with the Pandits was natural justice, according to me. If this had not happened, something else would have. For how long can ninety per cent people stay quiet on this. When I say all this now the Pandits get offended. But we must see our own filth too. What would pushing the blame serve? Now, you understand it like this: there is a body—the worker class is its feet, its stomach is the middle class and head is the intellectual class. The Pandits were just the head. It is easy to decapitate that. Had the Pandits also been in the stomach and the feet, it would have been difficult to separate us so.'

I was quiet.

'You also must be thinking that this Pandit has lost it.'

'Not at all, we must keep talking about our own drawbacks.'

'See, even now, the facts are that only ten per cent people are fighting for independence, and they are leaning towards Pakistan. Another ten per cent also fight for freedom but know that siding with Pakistan would be suicidal. The remaining eighty per cent sway to whichever side appears to have more clout.'

Jeevan's narrative had the flavour of tales, but those tales in which one could smell a bit of imagination mixed with facts. When I came back to my room, I felt numb. I could not make sense of anything. How much does each person have to say? Everybody in the Valley has so many stories, and there is bitterness too, because there is nobody who listens. If these stories can get some ears, maybe the restlessness of their narration would find some peace. I thought I must ask Jeevan if I could meet Usman.

The last time around I had missed the entrance of Khwaja Bagh. This time I was more alert. I was aware that there won't be a colony gate but a wall. I had decided that I would first go to my house and spend a lot of time there. I shall meet Kaka, and then call Baby Aunty and go to meet her. We were close because the same eucalyptus trees were visible now. I could hear my father's voice. 'We are almost home.'

'We are almost home.' I said this as if I was saying this for the very first time, as if these words are not related to my childhood in any way.

'Yes, just five minutes,' the driver said.

Roohani, too, was very excited. I was again looking out of the window. Six years! Would the blue door still be blue or would its blue have faded now? The white walls that were full of cracks, would they have not collapsed by now? This time I could not call my father for something like a permission to enter. His number, though, is still in my phone. I would call him on reaching the door and when nobody would pick at the other end, I would assume he didn't take my call.

I had written in my play *The Man with the Yellow Scooter*, 'Many things in life are like the problems of mathematics in which one has to begin with "Let's assume that".'

'Sir, we have crossed Khwaja Bagh. Where is your house?'

'Oh! We passed by again!'

The same thing happened all over again. The driver turned the car around, and I was once again standing in front of the bazaar of Khwaja Bagh. Then I looked at the walls. The walls had changed in six years. There were many advertisements painted on them. Behind the wall I couldn't see any tin roofs. I suddenly felt my legs becoming lighter—they couldn't bear the weight of my body. I sat on the ground. When the news of the demise of someone extremely dear to you reaches you, it feels as if someone is shouting loudly in your ears. Your entire body tries to cope with that loud cry inside, as if someone is draining everything out of you.

'Are you okay? What happened?'

Roohani was standing next to me. For a while I couldn't hear anything. The driver also came out of the car. I somehow again sat in the car.

'It is in the lane across. Take the car there.'

We entered the lane from the gate that we used to pass to steal apples when we were kids. The big gate there was missing; the wall around it had been demolished. I got out of the car and peeped inside; it felt as if I was looking at a construction site in Mumbai. There were workers all around, and several new buildings were being made. There was no sign of the old colony. I walked swiftly to the house at the end of the lane. There was no lane to walk—there was no ground left. It was difficult to find where the white walls and blue door that I had seen six years ago would be. There were big bulldozers and dust all around, and noise of hammering and cutting filled the air. Rooh was right six years ago when she had said, 'Please stay a little longer. You don't know if you will be able to come here again.' I could not come. I came to know the colony had been demolished a few years ago, and now new homes were being constructed here.

I had a strange thought: A few years ago, my father passed away, and around the same time, maybe the blue door and white walls were beaten into dust and demolished. Were my father and the home at Khwaja Bagh actually one? Were both bound to go at the same time? And I would never be able to stay a while longer with both of them in this lifetime. I wish I had not come out of the house six years ago; I wish I had picked up that call from my father. I wish I had gone straight back to him and asked him to smell me and take in the fragrance of his home from me.

I don't know how many places there are, where I could have stopped a little longer. My mother used to say that, as is common parlance, I have springs in my feet, that I can't stay for long at one place. I just wanted to stay in this moment; I had come here to stay.

I just wanted to hold on to something, wanted to hug someone with all my instability. I went to Kaka's house in the colony too, where his house could have been. The stumps of the new homes had grown in all the places, in all their ugliness. I would alternatively take two steps towards Kaka's house and two towards mine, all the colours of the old houses had faded in this haze.

After coming out of the colony I called Baby Aunty. She said, 'You wait there. I will send Gagandeep over.' Roohani was standing next to me; she wiped my face with her *odhni*.

'I am sorry I involved you in my personal journey, and I am not even worrying about what you must be feeling about this.'

Roohani didn't think it was appropriate to answer this. She just held my hand in both her hands and pressed it tight. Gagandeep was coming towards us on a bike. When I had seen him the last time he had been very young. He said, 'Come, Ma is waiting for you.'

Our car followed his bike. As soon as we reached home, we saw Baby Aunty standing on the stairs. Like I had seen the broken blue door and the dilapidated white walls six years ago, and tried to find some signs of the home I had lived in, I looked at Baby Aunty in the same way. As soon as I got close to her, she embraced me. I could feel her entire remaining strength in the grasp in which she held me. 'Our colony has been destroyed,' I said, and she looked at me. I tried to stop, but watching the parental affection in her eyes, I became a child and began to cry as much as I could.

In 2005, when the house had fallen during the earthquake, Baby Aunty was still living there. She was buried under the debris. A wall had also collapsed on Gagandeep, but the walls of that house were so thick that nobody lost their life.

'Her back has become better now,' Gagandeep said.

I noticed that Baby Aunty's hands were all over my body, constantly touching me.

'After you texted, I couldn't sleep all night. I would look at the message again and again to be sure that it was from you. I felt that you would run into my arms and cling to me just like you used to run and embrace me when you were a child.'

Then she got up suddenly and began to make parathas in the kitchen.

'Kaka was also here six years ago. Where is he now?'

Baby Aunty stopped rolling the paratha.

'Son, Kaka passed away some time ago due to Covid.'

'Covid?'

'Yes, his wife went back to Srinagar with their child, and his brother Suresh is in Ladakh maybe.'

Kaka was just a year older than me. I tried hard to remember his face. I tried, but I could remember only the people who looked like him, not him.

After having the paratha I saw some *malai* on the milk. I took a bowl and had some malai-shakkar (cream mixed with sugar). This had become my habit in Khwaja Bagh. Even today, if I see milk cream in anybody's house, I can't stop myself. Baby Aunty would look at me every few moments, as if she was seeing me for the first time. She must also be looking for that person in me whom she had been waiting for since yesterday. Do I have anything left in me from that time? Each touch from here was like the dense, protective shade of parental affection, and my entire being was covered in the dust of the city. I went to the bathroom at least thrice. I got this habit from my father. Whenever I could not stop myself, I would go to the bathroom for a little while longer.

The last time around I had not stayed in my house for long. This time I stayed with Baby Aunty for as long as I could.

On our way back, Roohani said, 'I felt as if I was instantly a part of some live documentary. I liked Baby Aunty a lot. So full of love!'

I was again looking at the tall white trees. I felt as if I was seeing them for the last time. Now, I will not have dreams of the blue door and the white walls. Maybe I will now dream of rubble. Just then I was reminded of my dream in which I was in my colony, but I couldn't reach my home. On our way back to Gulmarg, I kept lying down, with my head in Roohani's lap. There was nothing to see from the window of the car now.

A home crumbles right in front of the eyes
The closer we get to try and salvage it
The farther away it seems to be

All we see in its rising dust
Is the making and unmaking of faces

Where do the wrinkles on the face begin?
And where do the cracks of the home end?
The difference between them keeps getting hazier

When he was collecting his father's remains from the ashes
He found the remnants of his home therein . . .

My second meeting with Jeevan happened in the presence of one of his friends. His friend belonged to a family of rich merchants—one of the richest Muslim families of the Valley. They owned the first Mercedes in the Valley. They belonged to Sopore but were now living in Srinagar.

'I had heard that after 1989, a lot of rich Muslims also had to flee from the Valley. So how did you stay safe?' I asked a direct question right after the courtesies.

Meanwhile, Jeevan had ordered chai and girda for us. 'How were we safe? They abducted my younger brother and kept him in a small hut in a village for long. Then they agreed after a lot of negotiations. This means they could reach anywhere—home, factory, shop.'

'So you paid a ransom?'

'Everyone did. After you people had left, the condition of the people here was miserable. I would go to meet my Pandit friends in camps in Jammu. I have had meals several times with them. I agree their condition was terrible, but the conditions back here were even worse.'

Every few minutes, in the middle of the conversation, he would stick his tongue out, touch his ears and remember his Allah. The images of the situations of those times forced him into silence often.

'We would leave home not knowing whether we would return alive. You know, a Kashmiri throwing a kangri at someone was considered equivalent to someone throwing a bomb. A long time ago, somebody drew a knife in a brawl in a Sikh's sweet shop, and that remained a big incident for many years to come. This community had never witnessed violence of this nature. And who were we? We were all converted Muslims. Most had converted to Islam later, so we were all originally Pandits. That is why when you make a Kashmiri Sikh, a Muslim and a Hindu stand together, they all look the same.'

He was Jeevan's schoolfriend, and their jokes were from that time. 'I went to Amritsar in November to deliver orders for a Japanese company. When I came back to Kashmir in December, I saw that all the streets were empty, buildings had been burnt down, and the BSF and police were all over. I asked my driver what had happened to Kashmir. He said an evil eye had been cast on the Valley. The situation was very bad. In January, the situation became so bad that I was unable to recognize if this was the same heaven that I had left a few months ago. What happened after you left was that Muslims started killing each other. This became a struggle between the poor and rich, instead of a freedom struggle. And the funding that was happening, oh God! Every big country was sending funds here. Survival for people like us was tough. You can't even imagine the amount of money some people made. People who were workers and poor before, now have plenty of money and land. You ask them where they got all this from, and they have no answers.'

His wife was a Pakistani, who would add something sweet to the salty noon chai. Jeevan had laughed a lot at this. I would be reminded of Rooh often. She had said, if everyone here was good, then where was the person whose father had looted others? This is a fact that war and unrest are beneficial, too, for many. Kashmir has been a witness of this for thirty years.

'The removal of Article 370 was a good move; it should have been done years ago. But after that, the way the Kashmiris are being oppressed . . . I don't know how that is going to impact everything. In addition, what happened in Afghanistan is also going to have its implications for Kashmir. I don't know what lies ahead for Kashmir.'

He became quiet after mentioning Allah.

'I understand that any kind of extremist ideology is dangerous. We can at least learn this much from history,' I said.

'We do not know what might happen. We do not understand what is happening, and what has happened cannot be discussed. It is just a subject of arguments. This is Kashmir,' Jeevan added, and after that we returned to lighter conversation for an evening meet-up.

But I couldn't return; even today, my head becomes heavy after such conversations. I cannot listen to one kind of thing for long. Nobody has any solutions for such issues, and after a while the frustration begins to show on everyone's faces.

'The things that had started the trouble in Kashmir are now left far behind. Now it has become a paradox, from which just agents and middlemen are making money,' Jeevan's friend said to me in between our light conversation. 'When the Pandits left they thought that the rest of India would welcome them with open arms. And the Muslims thought that when they would chase the Pandits away and speak about freedom, Pakistan would embrace them warmly. But what happened finally was that neither of them was given any importance. Kashmiris became a football, and the people of the country cheered loudly, but it was a football being kicked from both sides, and nobody cared about this.' I don't know who said all this in the gathering. I was extremely tired and wanted to go back to my room.

When I returned to my room I sat down to write again. I looked for a long time at the words on my laptop that I had just written. But I was happiest about the fact that I was able to lend a listening ear to the people who needed it the most. I was trying to record what I had heard from them with the utmost honesty. At the beginning of writing this book, I also had various kinds of personal fears, questions and grievances, but they have all been left behind. Right now, if someone asks me what I want to ask, I would not have even a single question. There is no space for questions here. After coming here, one needs to experience the state of mind that stands with great difficulty to welcome you with thousands of unheard stories and rugged history.

I had some support from Roohani and the beautiful music of her violin; otherwise, it would have been difficult for me to go back to the cold mountains of Gulmarg. But we couldn't stay for long in Gulmarg, and we came back to Srinagar. I still didn't have the courage to return to Mumbai. It was impossible to go so far so quickly from here. I decided to spend a few days in Srinagar. Roohani, too, didn't want to return, so she stayed back with me in Srinagar. She might have been aware of the turmoil inside me and some sort of sympathy too. She said, 'You are in love with the violin, and therefore I will have to stay.'

Now any type of conversation with anyone about Kashmir would fill me with a strange restlessness. The moment I heard similar dialogues I just wanted to run away from there. I wanted to speak about my home, about Khwaja Bagh, about Kaka's demise, about my not staying there longer. Now, I also had a story, but there was nobody here who would listen to it. I began to walk. My aim was to reach the house at Rainawari by any means possible. If I walked fast, the sound of my footsteps hit my ears, as if there was someone else walking there instead of me; and if I walked slowly, it seemed as if I didn't want to reach anywhere at all. The Valley was now dipped in a colour of alienation. This wasn't the Kashmir I had entered into, and I too had become something else.

I wish I could see my Rooh on my way home, peeping from an old window of an ancient Kashmiri house. What would happen? Would I recognize my Rooh? And she would ask, 'Where are you going?'

'Home,' I would say.

'Where is home?' she would ask.

'Here, at the turn on the lane, there is a school, up ahead from there.'

'You come up,' she would say.

'How? I can't see any stairs,' I would say, and Rooh would start laughing. I wouldn't be able to go up, but Rooh would come down.

'Now that I have come down, let's go,' she would say.

'Where?'

'To your home.'

We would both walk into the turn on the lane, and we would see the school where children would be fearlessly reciting the Urdu alphabet, '*Aleph, be, pe, te, se* . . .' loudly. We would both turn, and the Rainawari home would appear in our vision. The tin door of the outer wall of that home . . . we would open it. Above us, in the deep-

blue sky, worn-out eagles would be hovering. As soon as we entered
that home, Ma would show us the cabbage planted in the front yard.
At each window there would be someone. Kids would be playing in
the open spaces between houses. I would be ignoring all of them and
looking for someone.

'Who are you looking for?' Rooh would ask me.

'I can't see my father,' I would reply to her.

'He lives in the Khwaja Bagh home,' Rooh would say.

Just then, we would find a secret pathway behind the house
leading up to Khwaja Bagh. We would both head out on that path, as
if we were just going for a stroll.

'I had always wished to touch these mountains,' Rooh would say
looking at the mountains on our way.

'I wanted to learn about every chaiwala's life.'

She would laugh at what I had said, touching a tree, and I would
kiss her under every tree. Can we not spend our entire lives on this
secret path? On reaching Khwaja Bagh, we would see my father
working on the road. Both of us would rush to him. I would ask,
'What are you doing?'

'I found the big gate of our colony in the Jhelum River. I am
trying to put it back in place of the wall,' he would say.

'Why?' I would ask.

'So that you don't lose your way if you ever come here again.
Walls have been raised everywhere in Kashmir.'

'But how will you demolish the wall? Where are the tools for it?'

He would show me his hands, with which he had been scratching
the base of the wall. I would see blood clots in his fingers that had
turned black.

'You are bleeding,' I would say.

'This is old blood that has clotted. You have new blood,' he
would say.

I would sit on my haunches on the wall on which my father
would be working. I would keep my Rooh on my shoulders instead
of my innards and pray that the wall wouldn't fall. There was no

colony behind it, the home was gone. I didn't want my father to find out that there was nothing behind this wall now.

People lie that time moves at its own pace. In reality, time sometimes runs slow and sometimes it moves swiftly. Time has its own empty circles. Each circle has its own time and its own speed.

'Have you seen the sky of Khwaja Bagh?' Rooh would stay, sitting on my shoulders.

I would look up and see white clouds and a little bit of blue sky peeping out of them.

'I remember this scene,' I would say. 'This is what was visible from the window of the house.'

The white clouds would seem like walls and the blue sky peeping out of them like a door.

'Don't put up the colony gate,' I would request my father.

'Why?'

'Because they will get it walled again. I will, instead, get a window, and we can put that up,' I would say this, but Father would ignore what I had said. I would rush to find the window in the rubble of the colony. I would leave my Rooh behind with my father at the wall. Some broken pieces of the window would be scattered there. I would gather them and reach Rooh. But there would be no Rooh there, no father, no wall. Hassled, I would arrange the pieces of wood in the shape of a window. Then I would peep inside it and see the wall hidden behind it, behind which Rooh would be eating something. I would call out and when she would turn around, her hands and mouth would be full of blood. She would get scared and begin to cry. I would see the remains of my father in front of her. I would push, I don't know who. The blue sky and wall would come crumbling down in front of me.

In the lanes of Srinagar, I was walking looking at the houses around instead of looking at the path ahead. Then I would stop at any random shop for a while and have tea. When I would overhear people speaking in Kashmiri, even though this was just an assumption, I would feel I was a part of these conversations. Some people would just look at me with a smile; some would try to strike a conversation. Those whom I didn't know felt the closest to me. Again and again, my gaze would move up to the sky, and I would see an eagle flying in circles. I would enter all strange lanes and greet every stranger with a smile. I would collect the replies carefully in my pocket. All that each one of us needs is this much affection.

When I was returning, I could hear the sound of the violin in the distance. Roohani was playing a symphony by Mozart at a slow pace. She had not noticed me entering the room. I sat at a corner of the bed and kept watching her. She was deeply engrossed in the music. I looked at my laptop lying in a corner. I felt the need to record this word 'rapt'. I opened the laptop and, instead of the word 'rapt', began to record these days hanging in between the emptiness. But what can be written about these days? How can these days ever be recorded even? I kept observing a lot of empty, meaningless words being typed, and then, when I was unable to see any more, I closed the laptop. This time Roohani had noticed my movement and put the violin down. There was now pin-drop silence in the room. I knew what I wanted to do in that moment. I wanted to make love to Roohani, so much love that everything would be washed off in the sweat of our bodies. She extended her hand and pulled me towards herself, and began to find a space inside her to hide me.

I was sitting at the window. Roohani brought coffee. We kept observing the changing reflections of the city in the lake all night long.

'Do you want to roam alone even today?' Roohani asked.

'No.'

'Then what's the plan today?'

'Since we didn't sleep all night, we shall sleep for a while.'

We both talked a bit more about sleeping. But neither I nor she moved away from the window. The sun was rising. The cold of last night trapped in the lake was now escaping as vapour. Neither I nor Roohani wanted to turn our faces from so much natural beauty and close our eyes for sleep.

'So, what is Kashmir for you now?'

'If we remove the people and overlook the human interventions, beautiful Kashmir always stands welcoming with open arms in all its beauty. This is like a deodar tree that is a thousand years old.

The head bows in reverence at its art of still standing straight. But this is not my Kashmir; this is not even the Kashmir of the people living here. This is nobody's Kashmir. This is just Kashmir, the one that remains in all its majestic beauty devoid of everything that is human. Seldom have I been able to see the glimpses of this Kashmir. This is also what surprises me that in spite of the fact that so much has occurred, these glimpses of Kashmir from unexpected corners are still very enticing.'

'I wish we could stay longer,' Roohani said.

'I was also thinking of the same. What is Kashmir for you?'

'After coming here, I feel I am far away. This feels like a part of some other planet. When I speak to my folks back home it seems they are asking me questions about this planet from the earth. As soon as the calls get disconnected all relationships end, as if they never existed. Even my violin plays a different tune here. It wasn't as melodious before. When I had thought of solo travel I wanted to get lost. Now I feel like I didn't want to exactly get lost but get closer to myself. I wanted to flow sitting at a spot, where I had to make no effort at all to wander . . .'

She had become quiet without completing what she had to say.

I thought that if Roohani wrote her travelogue, how engaging it would be! Without the information about Kashmir, without the opinion of people, that would have been the Kashmir whose glimpses one sees here and there. I had aimed to write about Kashmir, but I didn't have Roohani's vision. I have far too many lenses on my eyes. Was I able to see even once the Kashmir she sees? I was envious of Roohani's Kashmir. The Kashmir she is seeing is actually the Kashmir from my childhood that I am trying to get a hold on.

I saw she had fallen asleep, with the sun filtering in through the window. I pulled the curtains. Lying next to her, I began to think about my dream, and I began to wonder how the white walls and blue door might look in the snow. Even after thinking for long, all I could see was pitch blackness.

We went out in the afternoon. We reached Dal Gate number sixteen by a rickshaw, and then we took a shikara to Gulshan Book

Store. I was fortunate that Roohani was also deeply interested in books. We both wanted to step out of the room. The writing on Kashmir had concluded in my head. Many people ask me this: How do I know that the story is complete at a point? The truth is, I never come to know. Like when a relationship is closer to its end, you stop touching that person. You both wait for the last hug. I was also awaiting my last embrace with my writing on Kashmir, and yet I wanted to touch it over and over again. I opened my laptop as soon as we sat at the Gulshan Café, but I was afraid to touch it. Is it over now? What about the last embrace? Why is nothing evident of the nature of the final farewell?

At Gulshan Café, Roohani handed over a flask to me. I took a sip, it was vodka.

'What is this?' I blurted.

'It is our last day. We must celebrate.'

In a while, we were laughing at everything at Gulshan Café. After drinking I realized how badly we needed an afternoon like this one. Writing demands a lot of concentration. If while travelling the writer appears like a traveller, even then he remains outside of his writing. He should always witness the travel from within his writing. Everywhere I ask the questions, and he would gather the answers. And all of this has a peculiar fatigue. On such afternoons, the writer sleeps.

Just then my phone rang, it was an unknown number.

'Yes?' I asked.

'You want to meet Usman?' the voice at the other end asked.

'Usman?'

'Yes.'

'When?'

'Right now.'

'All right.'

'Write a number.'

I didn't know why I had started whispering. How quickly we succumb to bad acting. 'When do I have to call?' I asked after taking the number.

'Now.'

'All right.'

I was speaking to Jeevan, but I wasn't absolutely sure. In my bad attempt at acting like spy, I didn't even ask the name of the person before disconnecting the call. I immediately called Usman. For me, Usman's face was that of any young Kashmiri boy carrying a gun.

Some woman picked up the call. 'Yes, tell me?'

'May I speak with Usmanji.'

'Ji, who are you?'

When I told her my name she said, 'Here, speak to him.' I felt since I was too drunk, I was acting badly. Roohani was observing me through all this. She had seen Usman's name on the page and also his number against his name.

'Yes, please?'

'I had a long conversation with Jeevan about you. I wish to have a cup of tea with you.'

'Sure. Please come over.'

'Right now?'

'Yes, please write down the address.'

I wrote the address with shaky hands. This was the address of their party office.

'Should I come along?' Roohani asked.

'Of course, naturally.'

'But I know nothing about him.'

'I shall tell you on our way. But we shouldn't have drunk so much.'

As soon as I said this, we both laughed a lot.

'It seems like you have hit upon a treasure.'

'Your violin is playing in my head. It will be an interesting conversation, and I have a long list of questions. You know, after the 1993 blasts, Usman met Tiger Memon two–three times in Pakistan.'

'You will ask about that too?'

'No, I am just interested in Kashmir.'

I got a takeaway coffee from Gulshan Café to reduce the effect of the drinks.

'We are not so drunk. You are worrying too much.'

'For safety's sake, if I knew something of this nature would happen today, I wouldn't have drunk.'

'If we had known everything, then what would be the point of travelling?' Roohani said as we sat in the rickshaw, and I kissed her there itself.

'Oh! This is Kashmir.'

'Yes, that's why.'

I had finished my coffee by the time we reached their party office. There were banners and boards outside, and some people were shouting 'Zindabad'. We were asked to go to the office inside. A boy took us straight into a room where a lot of people sat in a circle. I found a vacant spot and sat there. I noticed Usman was sitting next to me. He had little hair on his head and a slight moustache; he was on the heavier side, eyes serious and big, and a smile on his lips. Just then I felt that all those people were uncomfortable, and the cause for that was Roohani. One girl was sitting among so many middle-aged men. Their gaze would often move towards her, but nobody said anything to her. I suddenly felt like laughing out loud, but I controlled myself. Then Usman told a man, 'Please take them to the room upstairs. I shall join them shortly.'

Roohani and I laughed a lot the moment we entered the room. Then tea and biscuits appeared, and we started waiting for Usman. In a while, Usman walked in speaking on the phone. There was a bearded man accompanying him. Usman asked him to call a few people and handed over his phone to this person. Now only three of us were in the room. Due to the vodka, Roohani and I were at the peak of our confidence. As soon as we were alone I began to ask him about his friends and his training in Pakistan. But he wanted to tell us how two web series were being made based on his life. The more my questions became serious, the more his answers became politically correct.

I tried to make it clear to him, 'I am not from the press. I am a fiction writer. I am writing this fictional travelogue of sorts. If you

insist, I shall change your name as well.' But Usman was clad in his
political costume firmly and rightly so. Admitting anything in front
of me would have been bad for him. Still, we did have a conversation
about many serious issues, though all his answers had been heard
before. This was just like extending what had been already said. I
began to lose interest in asking him any more questions. This wasn't
the Usman Jeevan and I had talked about. Though I was still curious
to know what had happened on his returning to Kashmir that made
him have a change of heart. He had first gone to the other side of
the border for six months and later for two years. He was a senior
member of the camp. He rubbed shoulders with the big shots of
the Pakistan Army. What happened then? I tried to ask this twice or
thrice, but every time he would start talking about his future plans
in politics. I wished to have tea with him, and that wish was fulfilled.
Before leaving, I told him that he could become the CM, that his
story had that strength. I knew he was interested in listening to
something of this nature. When we stepped out to similar-sounding
slogans being shouted out by similar-looking people, my head began
to get heavy. Roohani said she had felt sleepy during my conversation
with Usman.

'Do you have more vodka?' I asked.

'Yes, this is actually an opportune moment to have some.'

We walked to the Ahtus Hotel and filled the vodka we had in
a water bottle. We ordered haq and batt, which happens to be my
favourite Kashmiri dish, and we began drinking.

We left Ahtus quite drunk and unstable, and roamed in the lanes
around Lal Chowk. I was talking a lot, and Roohani would conclude
things with mere monosyllables.

'Are you okay?' I asked Roohani.

'I want to play the violin. Let's go back.'

Roohani had begun to sound like Rooh. She needed solitude. I
was listening to the sound of the violin from a distance.

The end of any journey, any relationship, drags us towards a loss
of words. All the conversations with Roohani had now dissolved
into silences. We could in no way understand relationships in this

manner. If one tries again to have a word about this relationship, it leaves a bitter taste in one's mouth. We were both fortunate that we had violin and Kashmir between us.

There were many messages from Shabeer: 'Please come over before you leave. Abbu keeps asking about you.' When I think about Shabeer, the thought of his father comes to my mind, as if his abbu had sent those messages. What would Mushtaq be doing now? When I was about to enter Kashmir, there were innumerable fears in me. Now, when it is time to leave, there is a moistness inside me.

'Can we stay for one more day?' Roohani asked.

'How?'

'You leave that to me.'

We were staying for a day more; there was somewhat of a last embrace left. We weren't exactly hungry to stay back; we were full, but our tongue wanted more, desired more. As we slipped away, we had to touch something a bit more, put it in our mouths. Now there was fragrance as well as taste, and at the next turn I would witness childhood—it was always a possibility.

I wanted to be left behind after this. On my last day in Kashmir, I wanted to stay like an empty boat in a still lake. In the notes of Roohani's violin melody, the influence of Kashmiri tunes was audible. I wanted to tell her, 'Your existence made being in Kashmir lighter.'

I had come here with so much of a fractured past. Before I'd met Roohani, it used to keep piercing me here and there, like a glass shrapnel. It pierced me in Roohani's presence too, but the pain had vanished. For Roohani, Kashmir begins where she opens her eyes. I could feel my attraction growing for her Kashmir.

I said, 'I want to keep roaming in your Kashmir on the last day here.'

'For that you will have to stop recording everything,' she said.

'I am ready.'

We crossed the lake in a shikara. When we reached the road, she stopped a rickshaw and asked the rickshaw driver, 'Would you take us to the old city?'

Both of us sat in the rickshaw.

'You are still recording.'

'No.'

'Don't lie.'

'I am sorry. I have a bad habit of writing continuously.'

'Leave it, or you won't be able to see anything.'

'All right, I have left it.'

The Itinerant Ghost

'A man will be imprisoned in a room with a door that's unlocked and opens inwards; as long as it does not occur to him to pull rather than push.'

—Ludwig Wittgenstein

Class eight exams had just concluded. It was about ten at night. He was unable to sleep. His father was supposed to be arriving in the morning. He thought about the Jhelum Express for a long time. He imagined that his father was some kind of a Betaal, and Jhelum was his horse, sitting on which he would cross several forests to reach here. Then he began to think about the wide shoulders of his father, how he would climb them and inhale his fragrance with deep breaths, till he was full of it. He had stomach worms, due to which he always remained hungry. He thought that only he catches that fragrance and only he can smell it. His gaze shifted to the clock—it was about to be eleven. His older brother was asleep, and Ma was putting the house in order inside. Whenever his father came, he felt it became colder. Maybe he'd brought Kashmir along with him.

Kashmir: blue sky and white clouds. He felt that actually his father smelt of Kashmir, yes, Kashmir. The moment he turned over he had an urge to pee. He didn't want to be in the bathroom when his father arrived. Hence, he was about to get up immediately but couldn't. Then he tried again to pee, but he could only change sides. He used all his strength. There was a loud cry, and then all became quiet.

Suddenly, he woke up. It was afternoon. He got up and went to the bathroom. The warmth of the afternoon could be felt through the bathroom window. He stood in front of the mirror. There was no hair on his head. Just a small braid—he had shaved his head at death.

Death?

He came out and saw he was in the hills. The entire forest had dried up. He looked around—it was Kashmir, deserted and desolate Kashmir. The sky was dipped in dewiness. As he walked further, leaves made a crumpling sound under his feet. He looked at the other side. He was walking by the Dal. There was very little water in the lake. It had turned black. The chinar trees in Char Chinar had dried up. Suddenly, he heard a voice—this was his father's voice. He was calling him. The voice was coming from the Mughal Gardens. He rushed to the Mughal Gardens to see his father standing in the water there and telling him to come quickly and climb on his shoulders for a picture to be clicked. He was slowly moving towards him. His father was saying that the water was so cold that his feet were becoming numb, so he must come quickly. He ran and jumped into the water. He shouted immediately; the water was actually very cold. He ran and clung to his father, and soon after he began to smell his father, the same fragrance. Absolutely the same! The fragrance of Kashmir. He was in Kashmir but the fragrance of Kashmir he got only from his father. So is it that the fragrance of Kashmir emanates from his father, or is it that his father's fragrance is spread all over Kashmir?

His father was wearing a red sweater from the Crocodile company. His white pajama was pulled up a bit as he was standing in water. 'Come on, quickly. Get on my shoulders, come on. I won't be able to stand for long . . .' his father said to him. His brother stood across from them with a Hotshot camera, saying, 'Come on, do it quickly. Can't you see Father is in so much discomfort?'

He quickly climbed on to his father's shoulders. His brother said, 'Adjust your sweater.' He noticed that it wasn't his father wearing the red sweater—he himself was wearing it. He looked at his father, who was wearing a white vest. His face was swollen and his lips had turned black. His gaze drifted to his father's stomach—it was bloated and hardening. His legs had begun to buckle. He shouted, 'Click it quickly, click!'

Just before his father fell, his brother could click the picture. A sharp light flashed before his eyes, and then everything went black.

His eyes began to burn. He couldn't keep them shut for long. When he opened his eyes he was in a small room. His hair was salt and pepper, and his beard was long. Ma was standing on the balcony wearing a white sari, and her phone was ringing.

'Ma, pick up the call,' he said.

'It's for you,' she said.

He picked up the phone. It was his father's voice on the other side. 'How are you, son? You didn't call. I was waiting. There was a match yesterday . . . congratulations! India won. Dhoni blasted them all,' his father said without a pause.

'Okay,' he said.

Father remained quiet for some time. He, too, didn't say anything.

'I was reading the newspaper,' he said. 'It has snowed today in Kashmir. Many soldiers are stranded.'

Again, some silence. Then Father said, 'Once I am better, we shall go to Kashmir. I shall take you. When are you coming? I have decided . . .'

He disconnected the call midway.

While serving tea Ma said, 'Speak to him. He will feel good. He keeps waiting for your call.'

'Okay, I will,' he said, ignoring his mother.

'When?' she asked.

'Whenever I get free.'

'What are you doing right now?'

'I am having tea.'

Ma remained quiet for a while. After the tea was finished, she said, 'Call him now.'

'I will.'

His mother kept looking at him. He kept looking back at her and then said, 'I am busy.' Then he stepped out and stood on the balcony. He kept looking at the wide expanse for a while. Two black crows came and sat on the tree in front of him. They were deep black in colour. Following them, two more crows came. Those were also the same colour. All four were looking at him. He found this quite strange. Just then there was a knock on the door.

'Ma, someone is at the door. Please check.'

Ma didn't reply to this. There was another knock. He turned around and saw that Ma was asleep. As he walked towards the door to open it, his footsteps created the sound of chinar leaves being crushed. He ignored that sound and walked towards the door. This time, the knocking was loud. The room was small, but he wasn't able to reach the door. He began to run, faster, and even faster . . . but the door still remained a few steps away.

Then he woke up. He saw that his mother and brother were asleep. Someone was knocking on the door. It was five in the morning. He uttered 'Papa' and lunged towards the door. As he opened the door, he saw the itinerant ghost standing there—Phantom. His white horse, Jhelum, was behind him and his dog, Sheru, beside him. He touched Phantom's feet and hugged him instantly. Phantom, too, smelt of Kashmir. He began to consume the fragrance. Phantom came inside with his two suitcases. He tried to wake his mother up, but Phantom asked him not to.

Phantom said, 'Close the door.'

He went to close the door, but the horse Jhelum or the dog Sheru weren't there now. Dawn was about to break. He was at an age when he raised no questions about any miracle. All miracles created the bubbles of confusion that would quickly disintegrate. By the time he turned his father had opened the suitcase. His mother was sitting next to him, and his brother was swinging on his shoulders. Father gave him a Cadbury chocolate, and he stepped out with it. The moment he was out a gush of cold wind hit him, and he closed his eyes.

When he opened his eyes he was in a government colony in Kashmir. There was snow all around, and the colony was now in ruins. He was being dragged towards the last house in the lane. In the veranda of the last house in the lane, Father was making snowballs. He had already made three balls and was making a fourth one, which he had rolled and put close to the other three. He sat on the parapet of the veranda and began to notice his father's exhaustion. Now, four balls were all kept in a row. He took out marbles from his pocket and made their eyes.

'How do they look?' his father asked him without looking at him.

'Are you asking me?' he said hesitatingly.

'Who else is present here?'

'It is looking good.'

Just then, the largest ball broke apart. He couldn't see it. He ran to gather the snow of that ball. The more he tired to put it together, the more it would fall apart. He saw his father sitting on the parapet. Four crows sat next to him—deep black. Now there were only three balls with eyes of marbles. He began to search for two more marbles in the snow.

'Why have you shaved your head?'

His father's voice rang from behind him, but he was frantically looking for the marbles.

'You are looking for my eyes?' his father asked.

He stopped. He saw his father was sitting on the parapet with a phone, dialling a number. The bell rang after a while. The phone that was ringing lay next to him. He ran and sat beside his father on the parapet and took the call. He heard his father's voice on the other side, 'Hello!'

'Papa, there should be four balls. Why has this one ball disintegrated? It shouldn't have broken now, there is snow all over. We had recently received relief from the intense heat. Lately, we have been happy together. It wasn't meant to disintegrate now!'

After saying this I looked at my father.

'Papa, I am unwell.'

Hearing this, his father began to look at him. They both had phones on their ears. His father disconnected the call and said to him, 'Why do you ride the yellow scooter?'

He saw that he was riding the yellow scooter fast in Bombay. His hair was salt-and-pepper, and his beard was long. He was going to receive his father from the station. It was morning. He saw a tea stall. He stopped the scooter. The tea vendor puts a cup of tea in his hand without even asking him. He was about to light a cigarette with the chai when the chai vendor asked him, 'Aren't you getting late?'

'No, late for what?' he asks.

'It is thirty-first January today.'

'Yes, so?'

'So, you see, I thought I must ask whether you were getting late?'

He drank the tea at leisure, but the thought about getting late remained in his mind. He looked for a watch, but he wasn't wearing any. He fumbled in his pocket for his mobile, but he didn't have that either. He asked the tea vendor, 'What's the time?'

'Not much time left.'

He kept the tea down, threw away the lit cigarette and, without paying the tea vendor, kicked his scooter to start it. The scooter didn't start. He looked at the tea vendor and was reminded that he hadn't paid. He paid the money, and the yellow scooter started. He set off swiftly for the station. His yellow scooter was running fast. The morning fog around him intensified; everything around him began to fade gradually. He felt cold in the dense fog. Then he heard the train's hooter. He could smell Kashmir around him. A station appeared in the fog ahead; the name of the station was Kashmir. He parked his scooter and rushed inside the station. On the morning of 31 January, the train wasn't arriving at the station but was departing. He wasn't late to receive his father but to drop him off. The train was leaving the station. From the window of the train he saw his father's hand. He saw 'OM' marked on that hand. He was waving his hand to bid him the final goodbye.

Immediately, the entire station and train vanished, and he saw that he was standing in a chinar forest covered in snow. There was a cigarette in his hand, and he was looking for something in the fog. Then he saw his father behind a chinar tree.

'How come you are here?' he asked.

'I was looking for my land. There is snow all around, and I am unable to make sense of anything,' his father said.

'Your land was lost long ago. Now, even if you are standing on your own land, you won't be able to make out if this is your own land.'

'I will come to know.'

'Everything has changed here.'

'But I haven't changed,' his father said and began to look for his land. Vapour emanated from their mouths as they talked. He came closer to his father.

'Papa, you went too early. A lot still remained.'

'What remained?'

'I don't know. Your part of the story?'

His father smiled.

'You are standing in my part of the story.'

Then he heard a horse's gallop. Jhelum emerged from the fog and stood next to his father. The moment his father jumped and climbed on to it, it became the itinerant ghost—Phantom.

Jhelum's gallop had moved far away from the train's sound.

He picked up his phone and called his father. It kept ringing for a long while, but there was nobody at the other end.